S0-BMZ-640

The Big Book Of
UNIQUE
SHAPES

Home décor has never been this easy! Using unique plastic canvas shapes, such as circles, hearts, stars, squares, and hexagons, you can stitch up 45 accents to fill your house with fun. Let your imagination take flight as butterflies flutter on magnets and towel holders for the kitchen. Spring is in bloom on coasters, a tissue box cover, and a photo frame. Animals abound on projects for kids' rooms — teddy bears, puppies, and kittens are sure to be adored! Young athletes will appreciate a sporty set of coasters, magnets, and a treasure chest. Make Baby's naptime heavenly with a moon-and-stars mobile, tissue topper, door sign, and switch plate cover. There's something to please everyone in the family! Have fun deciding which project to make first.

LEISURE ARTS, INC.
Little Rock, Arkansas

PRINTED WITH
SOY INK

Made in U.S.A.

1

The Big Book Of UNIQUE SHAPES

EDITORIAL STAFF

Vice President and Editor-at-Large: Anne Van Wagner Childs
Vice President and Editor-in-Chief: Sandra Graham Case
Director of Designer Relations: Debra Nettles
Editorial Director: Susan Frantz Wiles
Publications Director: Susan White Sullivan
Creative Art Director: Gloria Bearden
Photography Director: Karen Hall
Art Operations Director: Jeff Curtis

PRODUCTION
Managing Editor: Mary Sullivan Hutcheson
Production Editor: Merrilee Gasaway
Production Assistants: Jo Ann Forrest and Janie Marie Wright

EDITORIAL
Managing Editor: Suzie Puckett
Contributing Editor: Nancy Dockter

ART
Senior Art Director: Rhonda Shelby
Senior Production Artist: Lora Puls
Production Artist: Wendy Willets
Color Technician: Mark Hawkins
Photography Stylist: Tiffany Huffman
Publishing Systems Administrator: Becky Riddle
Publishing Systems Assistants: Myra S. Means and
   Chris Wertenberger

BUSINESS STAFF

Publisher: Rick Barton
Vice President, Finance: Tom Siebenmorgen
Vice President, Retail Marketing: Bob Humphrey
Vice President, Sales: Ray Shelgosh
Director of Corporate Planning and Development:
   Laticia Mull Cornett

Vice President, National Accounts: Pam Stebbins
Director of Sales and Service: Margaret Sweetin
Vice President, Operations: Jim Dittrich
Comptroller, Operations: Rob Thieme
Retail Customer Service Manager: Wanda Price
Print Production Manager: Fred F. Pruss

Copyright© 2001 by Leisure Arts, Inc., 5701 Ranch Drive, Little Rock, Arkansas 72223-9633. Visit our Web site at **www.leisurearts.com**. All rights reserved. No part of this book may be reproduced
any form or by any means without the prior written permission of the publisher, except for brief quotations in reviews appearing in magazines or newspapers. We have made every effort to ensure th
these instructions are accurate and complete. We cannot, however, be responsible for human error, typographical mistakes, or variations in individual work. Printed in the United States of America.

Softcover ISBN 1-57486-243-X

10   9   8

TABLE OF CONTENTS

Scent of Spring Birdhouse

A happy, little bluebird has come out of her house to enjoy the fresh scent of spring! Now you can, too, with this cheery potpourri holder. Just fill the birdhouse with your favorite scent and hang it by a window — what a fun-and-easy way to celebrate the season.

Skill Level: Intermediate

Size: 7"w x 6"h x 4½"d

Supplies: Worsted weight yarn (refer to color keys), one 10½" x 13½" sheet of clear 7 mesh plastic canvas, two 6" Uniek® plastic canvas heart shapes, four 3" Uniek® plastic canvas circle shapes, five 5" Uniek® hexagon shapes, a #16 tapestry needle, and an 18" length of white cord.

Stitches Used: French Knot, Gobelin Stitch, Overcast Stitch, and Tent Stitch.

Instructions: Follow charts to cut and stitch Birdhouse pieces, working French Knot last. Using white overcast stitches, join Bottom pieces along unworked short edges. Join Bottom to unworked edges of Front and Back, placing seam at inner point of hearts. Using pink overcast stitches, join Roof pieces along unworked short edges. Using white overcast stitches, join Eave to front edge of Roof. Using pink overcast stitches, cover remaining unworked edge of Roof. Join unworked edges of Perch Top and Bottom to Perch Side. Tack Perch to Front. Tack Wing to Bird; tack Bird to Front. Tack Leaves to Front and Roof. For each daisy, tack two Petals together; tack Centers to daisies. Tack daisies to Front and Roof. For hanger, thread cord ends through center of Roof; knot on wrong side of Roof. Securely tack Roof to Bottom, Front, and Back.

COLOR	
⬜	white - 60 yds
⬜	yellow - 1 yd
⬜	peach - 1 yd
⬜	pink - 41 yds
⬜	lt blue - 4 yds
●	*black Fr. knot - 1 yd
▬	cutting line

*Use 2 plies of yarn.

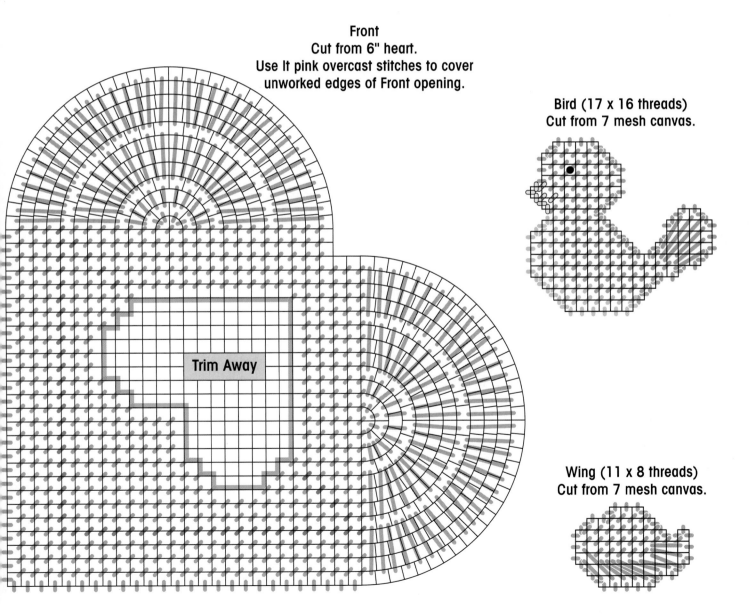

Front
Cut from 6" heart.
Use lt pink overcast stitches to cover
unworked edges of Front opening.

Trim Away

Bird (17 x 16 threads)
Cut from 7 mesh canvas.

Wing (11 x 8 threads)
Cut from 7 mesh canvas.

Eave (35 x 35 threads)
Cut from 7 mesh canvas.

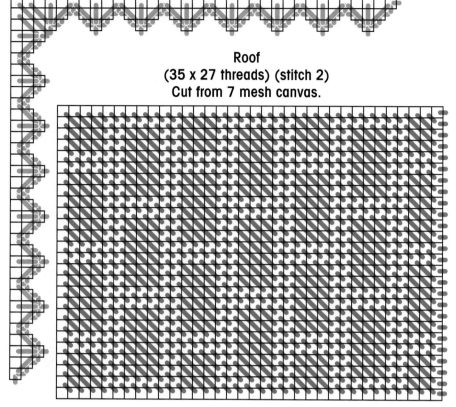

Roof
(35 x 27 threads) (stitch 2)
Cut from 7 mesh canvas.

	COLOR		COLOR
/	white	/	pink
/	yellow	/	green - 6 yds
/	lt pink - 10 yds	−	cutting line

Center (stitch 2)
Cut from 3" circles.
Use yellow overcast stitches to cover
unworked edges of Centers.

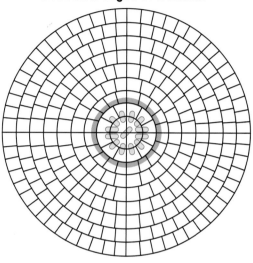

Petals (stitch 4)
Cut from 5" hexagons.
Use lt pink overcast stitches to
cover unworked edges of Petals.

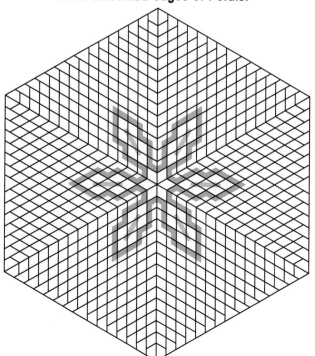

Leaves
Cut from 5" hexagon.
Use green overcast stitches to
cover unworked edges of Leaves.

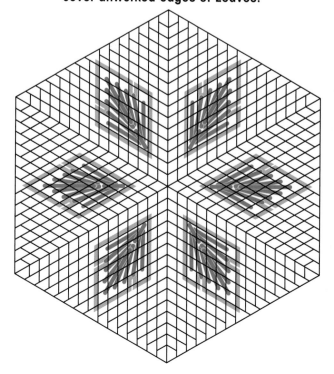

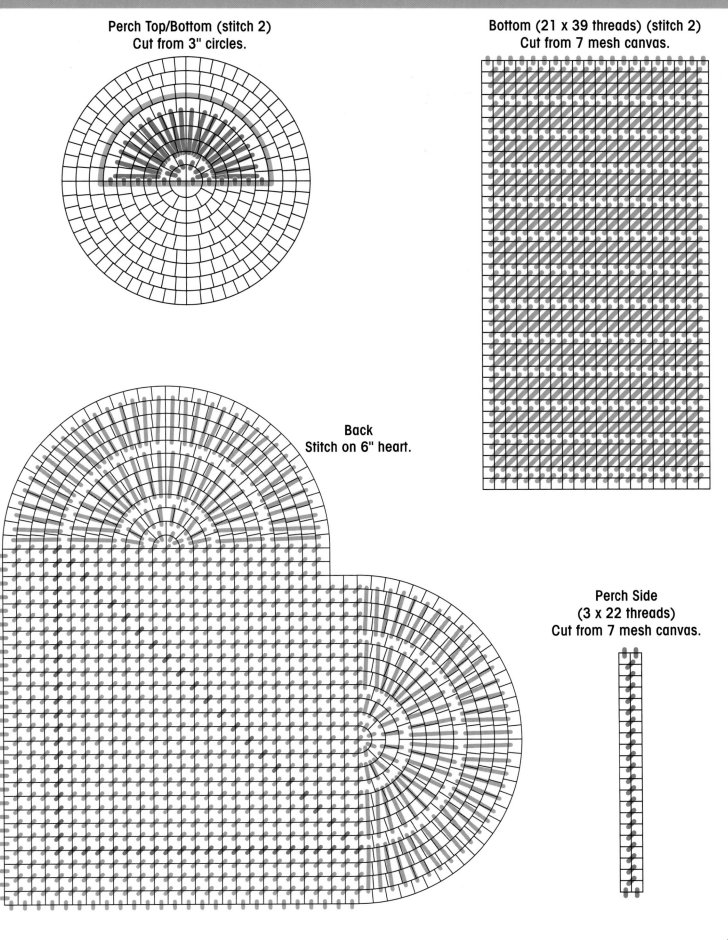

Perch Top/Bottom (stitch 2)
Cut from 3" circles.

Bottom (21 x 39 threads) (stitch 2)
Cut from 7 mesh canvas.

Back
Stitch on 6" heart.

Perch Side
(3 x 22 threads)
Cut from 7 mesh canvas.

Rose Coaster Bouquet

Protect your tabletops with timeless beauty by arranging this regal bouquet of rose coasters. A beribboned storage box completes the romantic set.

COASTER SET

Skill Level: Beginner

Coaster Size: 4"w x 4"h each

Holder Size: 4½"w x 2"h x 1½"d

Supplies: Worsted weight yarn (refer to color key), eight 4" Uniek® plastic canvas square shapes or two 10½" x 13½" sheets of clear 7 mesh plastic canvas, #16 tapestry needle, and a 21" length of ¼"w burgundy ribbon.

Stitches Used: Backstitch, Mosaic Stitch, Overcast Stitch, and Tent Stitch.

Instructions: Follow charts to cut and stitch Coaster Set pieces, working backstitches last. For Bottom, cut a piece of 7 mesh canvas 28 x 10 threads. Bottom is not worked. Using ecru overcast stitches, cover unworked edges of holes in Front, Back, and Sides. Join Front and Back to Sides. Join Bottom to Front, Back, and Sides. Thread ribbon through holes in Front, Back, and Sides; tie bow and trim ends.

COLOR		COLOR	
✎	ecru - 36 yds	✎	dk green - 10 yds
✎	lt pink - 17 yds	✎	*burgundy - 12 yds
✎	pink - 23 yds	▭	cutting line
✎	green - 17 yds		*Use 2 plies of yarn.

Side (10 x 14 threads) (stitch 2)
Cut from 4" square or 7 mesh canvas.

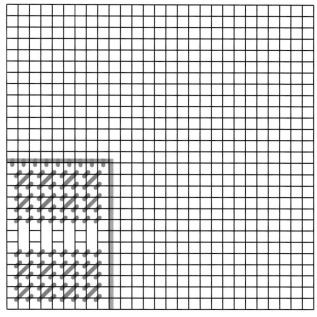

Front/Back
(28 x 14 threads) (stitch 2)
Cut from 4" square or 7 mesh canvas.

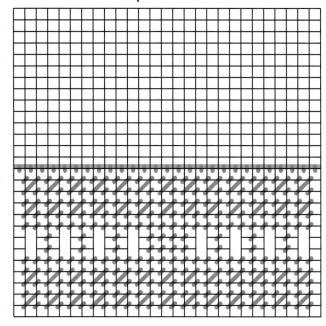

Coaster
(27 x 27 threads) (stitch 6)
Cut from 4" squares or 7 mesh canvas.

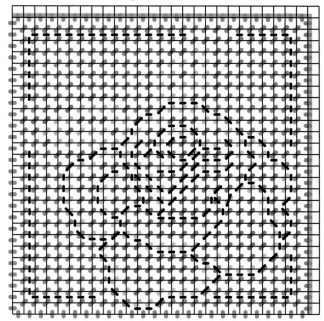

Floral Extravaganza

This floral extravaganza is a tribute to the wonders awaiting us outside. Abloom with perky petals, a tissue box cover, a doorhanger, and a boxed coaster set bring Nature's artistry into your home.

TISSUE BOX COVER

(Photo, page 10.)
Skill Level: Beginner
Size: 5"w x 6"h x 5"d
(Fits a 4¼"w x 5¼"h x 4¼"d boutique tissue box.)
Supplies: Worsted weight yarn (refer to color key), two 10½" x 13½" sheets of clear 7 mesh plastic canvas, three 5" Uniek® plastic canvas star shapes, #16 tapestry needle, and a 24" length of ¼"w white ribbon.
Stitches Used: Gobelin Stitch, Mosaic Stitch, Overcast Stitch, and Tent Stitch.
Instructions: Follow charts to cut and stitch Tissue Box Cover pieces. Using blue overcast stitches, cover unworked edges of holes on Top. Join Sides along long edges. Join Top to Sides. Thread ribbon through holes on Top; tie bow and trim ends. Tack Leaves and Flowers to Top and Side.

COLOR	
✎	white - 1 yd
✎	lt yellow - 2 yds
✎	yellow - 1 yd
✎	lt pink - 2 yds
✎	pink - 1 yd
✎	lt purple - 2 yds
✎	purple - 1 yd
✎	blue - 68 yds
✎	green - 8 yds
−	cutting line

Top (32 x 32 threads)
Cut from 7 mesh canvas.

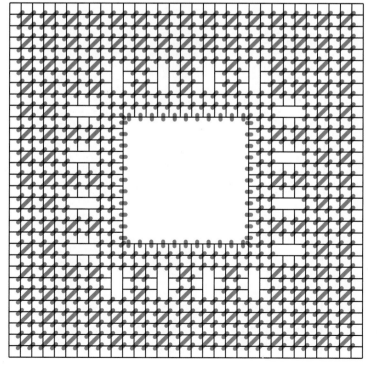

Side (32 x 38 threads) (stitch 4)
Cut from 7 mesh canvas.

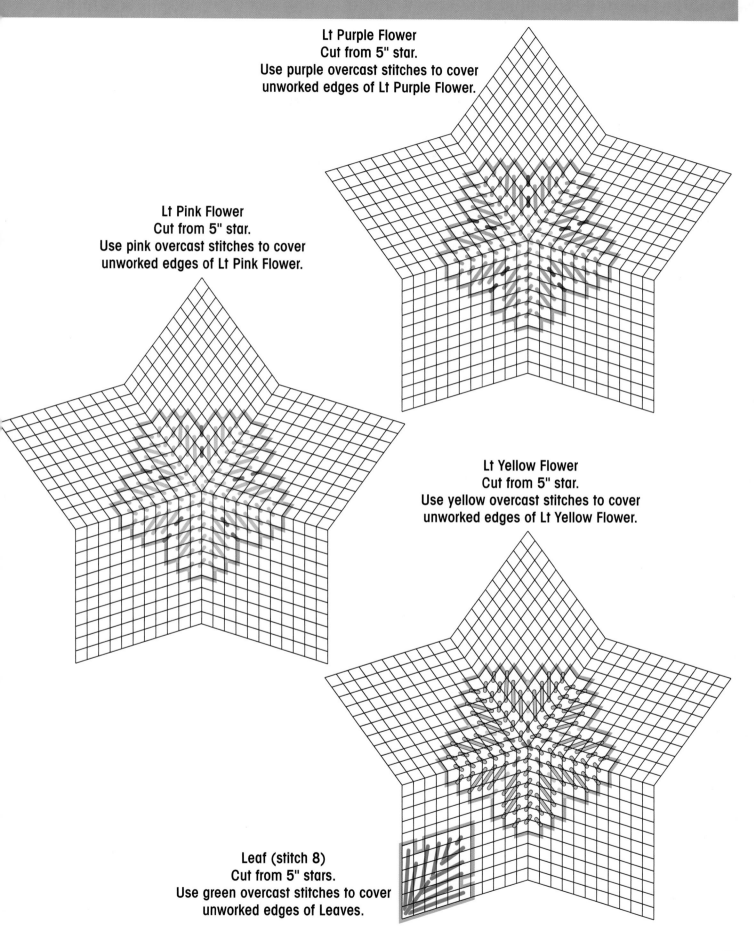

Lt Purple Flower
Cut from 5" star.
Use purple overcast stitches to cover
unworked edges of Lt Purple Flower.

Lt Pink Flower
Cut from 5" star.
Use pink overcast stitches to cover
unworked edges of Lt Pink Flower.

Lt Yellow Flower
Cut from 5" star.
Use yellow overcast stitches to cover
unworked edges of Lt Yellow Flower.

Leaf (stitch 8)
Cut from 5" stars.
Use green overcast stitches to cover
unworked edges of Leaves.

COASTER SET

(Photo, page 11.)

Skill Level: Intermediate

Coaster Size: 4"w x 4"h each

Holder Size: 5" dia.

Supplies: Worsted weight yarn (refer to color keys), one 10 1/2" x 13 1/2" sheet of clear 7 mesh plastic canvas, two 6" Uniek® plastic canvas circle shapes, one 3" Uniek® plastic canvas circle shape, seven 5" Uniek® plastic canvas star shapes, #16 tapestry needle, 16" length of 1/4"w white ribbon, and craft glue.

Stitches Used: Cross Stitch, Gobelin Stitch, Mosaic Stitch, Overcast Stitch, and Tent Stitch.

Instructions: Follow charts to cut and stitch Coaster Set pieces, leaving stitches in pink shaded areas unworked. For Top, match ▲'s and ■'s and work stitches in pink shaded area to join Top Side 1 to Top Side 2. Matching ♥'s and ★'s, work stitches in pink shaded area to join Top Side 2 to Top Side 1, forming a ring. Using blue overcast stitches, join Top to Top Sides along unworked edge. Tack Top Flower Petals to wrong side of Center; tack Center to Top. For Bottom, trim away four threads from the outer edge of remaining 6" circle. Bottom is not worked. Matching ▲'s and ■'s, work stitches in pink shaded area to join Bottom Side 1 to Bottom Side 2. Matching ♥'s and ★'s, work stitches in pink shaded area to join Bottom Side 2 to Bottom Side 1, forming a ring. Using blue overcast stitches, join Bottom to Bottom Sides along unworked edge. Thread ribbon through holes on Top Sides, glue ribbon ends to back of Top Sides.

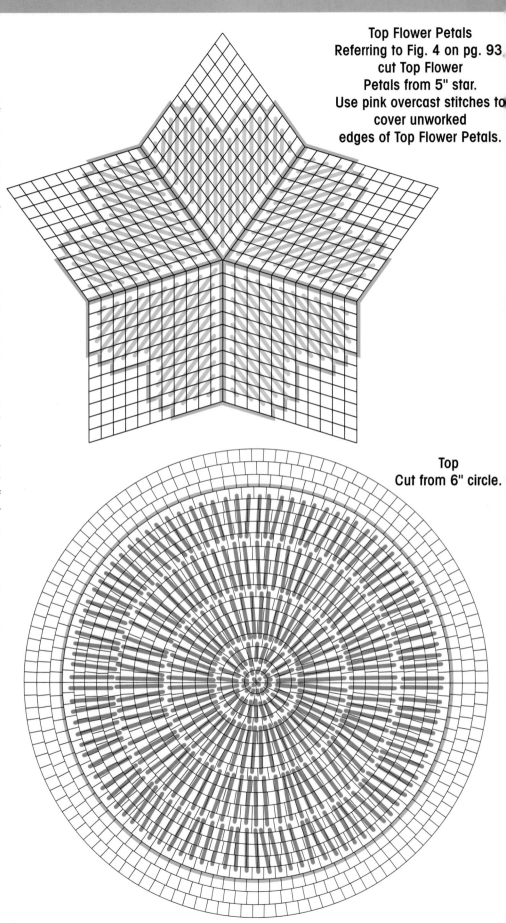

Top Flower Petals
Referring to Fig. 4 on pg. 93 cut Top Flower Petals from 5" star. Use pink overcast stitches to cover unworked edges of Top Flower Petals.

Top
Cut from 6" circle.

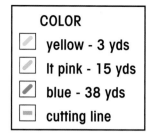

COLOR
- yellow - 3 yds
- lt pink - 15 yds
- blue - 38 yds
- cutting line

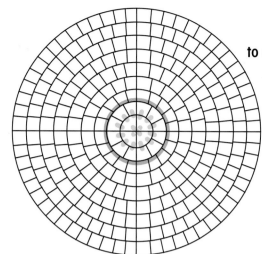

Center
Cut from 3" circle.
Use yellow overcast stitches
to cover unworked edges of Center.

Bottom Side 1 (48 x 12 threads)
Cut from 7 mesh canvas.

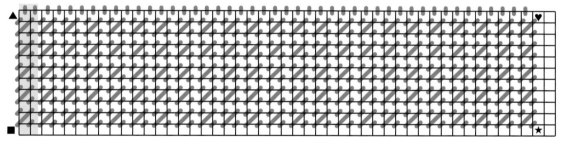

Bottom Side 2 (48 x 12 threads)
Cut from 7 mesh canvas.

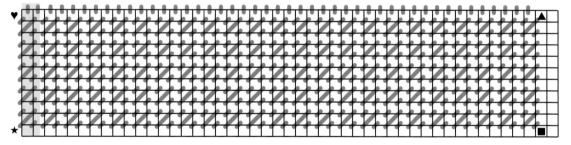

Top Side 1 (52 x 6 threads) Cut from 7 mesh canvas.
Use blue overcast stitches to cover unworked edges of holes in Top Side 1.

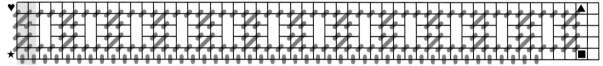

Top Side 2 (52 x 6 threads) Cut from 7 mesh canvas.
Use blue overcast stitches to cover unworked edges of holes in Top Side 2.

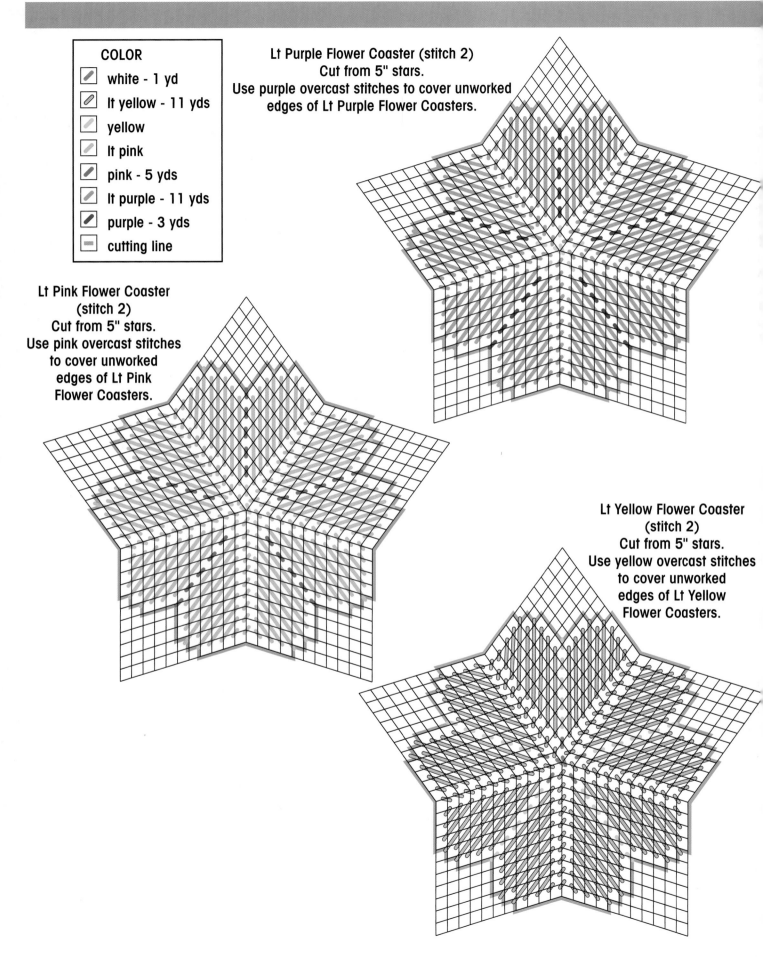

COLOR

- white - 1 yd
- lt yellow - 11 yds
- yellow
- lt pink
- pink - 5 yds
- lt purple - 11 yds
- purple - 3 yds
- cutting line

Lt Purple Flower Coaster (stitch 2)
Cut from 5" stars.
Use purple overcast stitches to cover unworked
edges of Lt Purple Flower Coasters.

Lt Pink Flower Coaster
(stitch 2)
Cut from 5" stars.
Use pink overcast stitches
to cover unworked
edges of Lt Pink
Flower Coasters.

Lt Yellow Flower Coaster
(stitch 2)
Cut from 5" stars.
Use yellow overcast stitches
to cover unworked
edges of Lt Yellow
Flower Coasters.

(Photo, page 11.)

Skill Level: Beginner

Size: 6³/₄"w x 5³/₄"h

Supplies: Worsted weight yarn (refer to color keys), two 6" Uniek® plastic canvas circle shapes, three 5" Uniek® plastic canvas star shapes, #16 tapestry needle, and 14" length of ¼"w white ribbon.

Stitches Used: Gobelin Stitch, Overcast Stitch, and Tent Stitch.

Instructions: Follow charts to cut and stitch Doorhanger pieces. Tack Leaves and Flowers to Front. Using blue overcast stitches, cover inner horizontal edge of Back. Join Front to Back along unworked edges. Thread ribbon through top of Doorhanger; tie bow and trim ends.

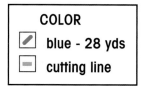

COLOR

✎ blue - 28 yds

⚊ cutting line

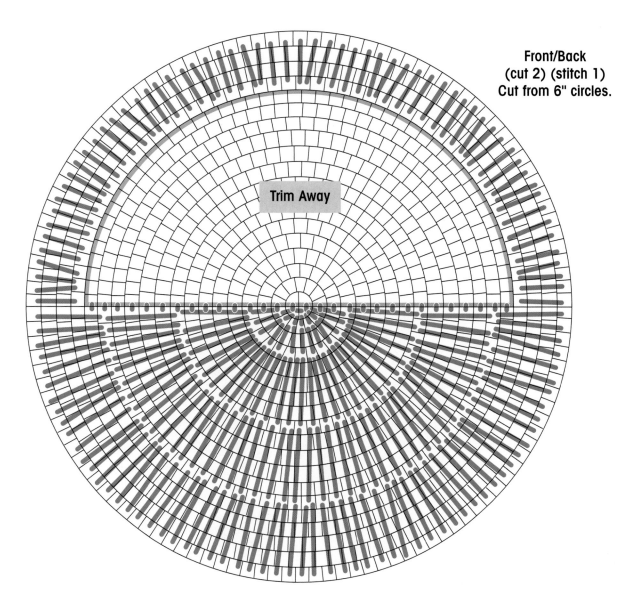

Front/Back
(cut 2) (stitch 1)
Cut from 6" circles.

Trim Away

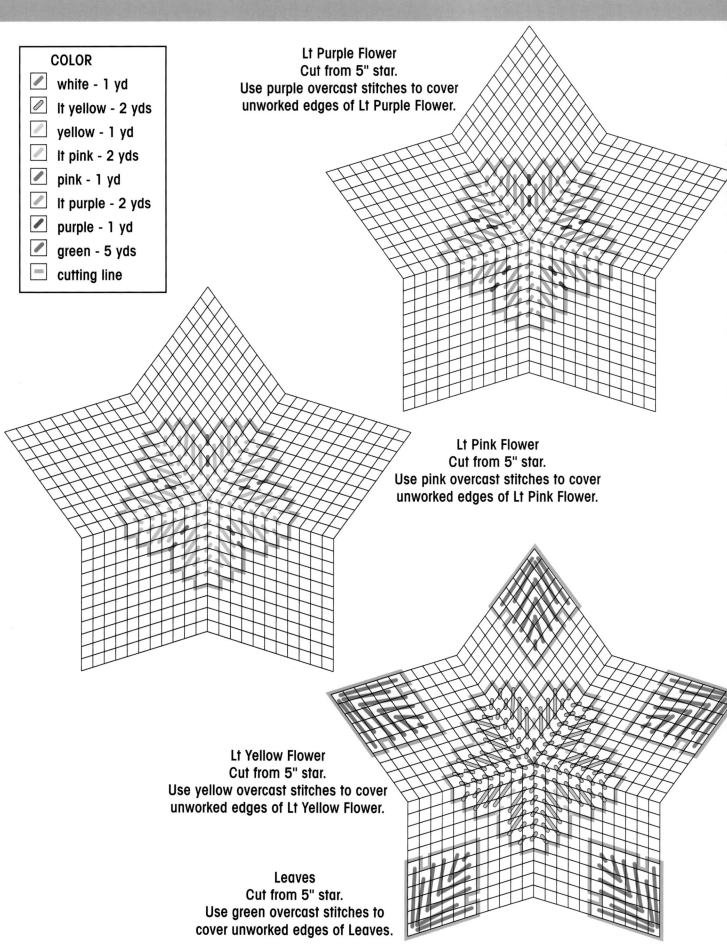

COLOR

✎	white - 1 yd
✎	lt yellow - 2 yds
✎	yellow - 1 yd
✎	lt pink - 2 yds
✎	pink - 1 yd
✎	lt purple - 2 yds
✎	purple - 1 yd
✎	green - 5 yds
▬	cutting line

Lt Purple Flower
Cut from 5" star.
Use purple overcast stitches to cover
unworked edges of Lt Purple Flower.

Lt Pink Flower
Cut from 5" star.
Use pink overcast stitches to cover
unworked edges of Lt Pink Flower.

Lt Yellow Flower
Cut from 5" star.
Use yellow overcast stitches to cover
unworked edges of Lt Yellow Flower.

Leaves
Cut from 5" star.
Use green overcast stitches to
cover unworked edges of Leaves.

Fresh as a Daisy Frame

This daisy photo frame is a sure pick for showing off the fresh innocence of your special little someone.
The oh-so-sweet keepsake will help you hold your loved one close to your heart.

FRAME

(Photo, page 19.)
Skill Level: Beginner
Size: 6³/₄"w x 6¹/₄"h
(Photo opening is 3¹/₄"w x 2³/₄"h.)
Supplies: Worsted weight yarn (refer to color key), one 10¹/₂" x 13¹/₂" sheet of clear 7 mesh plastic canvas, two 6" Uniek® plastic canvas heart shapes, four 5" Uniek® plastic canvas hexagon shapes, two 3" Uniek® plastic canvas circle shapes, and #16 tapestry needle.

Stitches Used: Gobelin Stitch, Overcast Stitch, and Tent Stitch.
Instructions: Follow charts to cut and stitch Frame pieces. For each daisy, tack two Petals together; tack Centers to daisies. Tack daisies to Front. Using blue overcast stitches, join Stand Front to Stand Back. Referring to Diagram, tack Stand to Back. Join unworked edges of Front and Back.

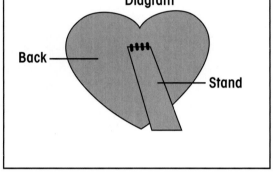

Diagram

Back

Stand

Center (stitch 2)
Cut from 3" circles.
Use yellow overcast stitches to cover unworked edges of Centers.

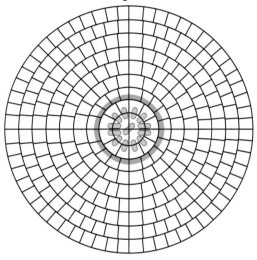

Petals (stitch 4)
Cut from 5" hexagons.
Use white overcast stitches to cover unworked edges of Petals.

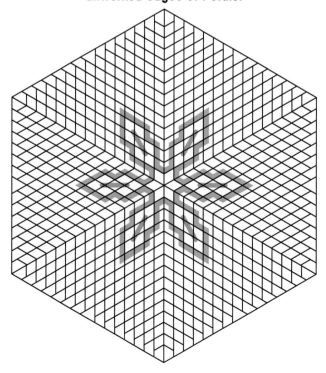

Stand Front/Back
(20 x 31 threads) (cut 2) (stitch 1)
Cut from 7 mesh canvas.

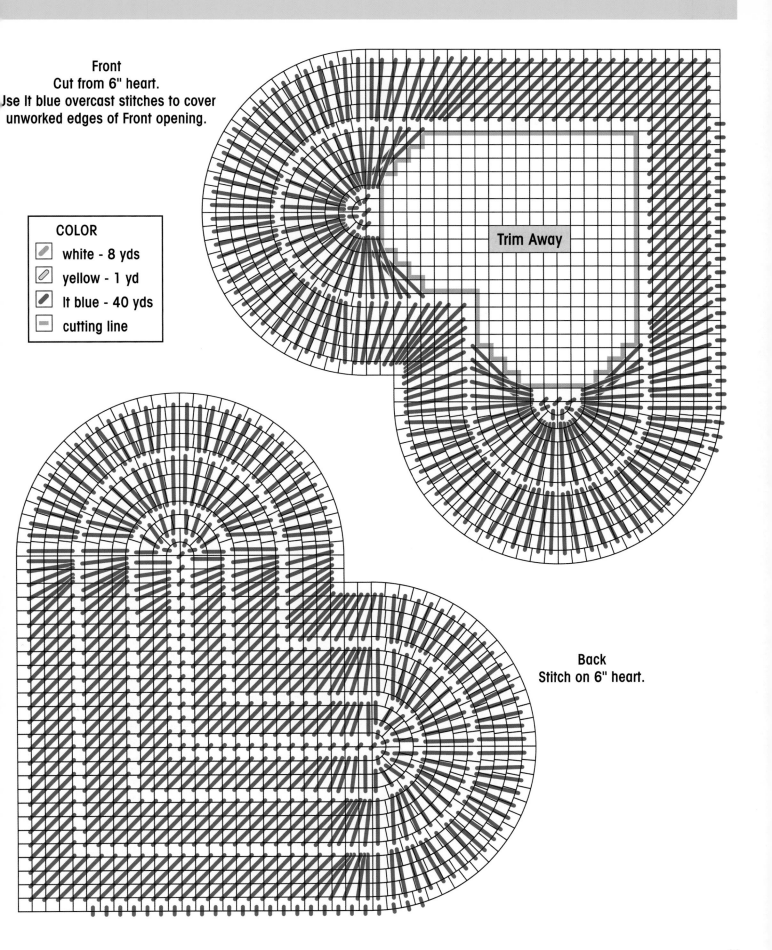

Front
Cut from 6" heart.
Use lt blue overcast stitches to cover
unworked edges of Front opening.

COLOR
white - 8 yds
yellow - 1 yd
lt blue - 40 yds
cutting line

Trim Away

Back
Stitch on 6" heart.

21

Winged Beauties

Stitch up this ensemble of butterflies to decorate your home inside and out. Let the winged beauties light on refrigerator magnets and easy-to-stitch towel holders to add a cheery touch to your kitchen. Ribbons flutter from whimsical windsocks to offer a friendly welcome to guests.

(Photo, page 23.)
Skill Level: Beginner
Towel Holder Size: 6¹⁄₂"w x 4¹⁄₄"h each
Magnet Size: 3¹⁄₄"w x 3¹⁄₂"h each
Supplies: Worsted weight yarn (refer to color key), one 10¹⁄₂" x 13¹⁄₂" sheet of clear 7 mesh plastic canvas, two 6" Uniek® plastic canvas circle shapes, sixteen 3" Uniek® plastic canvas circle shapes, #16 tapestry needle, eight 4" lengths of 6mm black chenille stem, magnetic strip, and craft glue.

Stitches Used: Gobelin Stitch, Overcast Stitch, and Tent Stitch.
Instructions: Follow charts to cut and stitch Towel Holder and Magnet pieces. For butterflies, use black overcast stitches to join unworked edges of Left and Right Wings to Body. Thread one chenille stem through each Body; trim ends. Tack two butterflies to each Towel Holder. Glue a magnetic strip to back of four remaining butterflies.

COLOR	
▧	yellow
▧	orange
▨	pink
▧	lt purple
▧	purple
▨	blue
▧	turquoise
▰	black
▭	cutting line

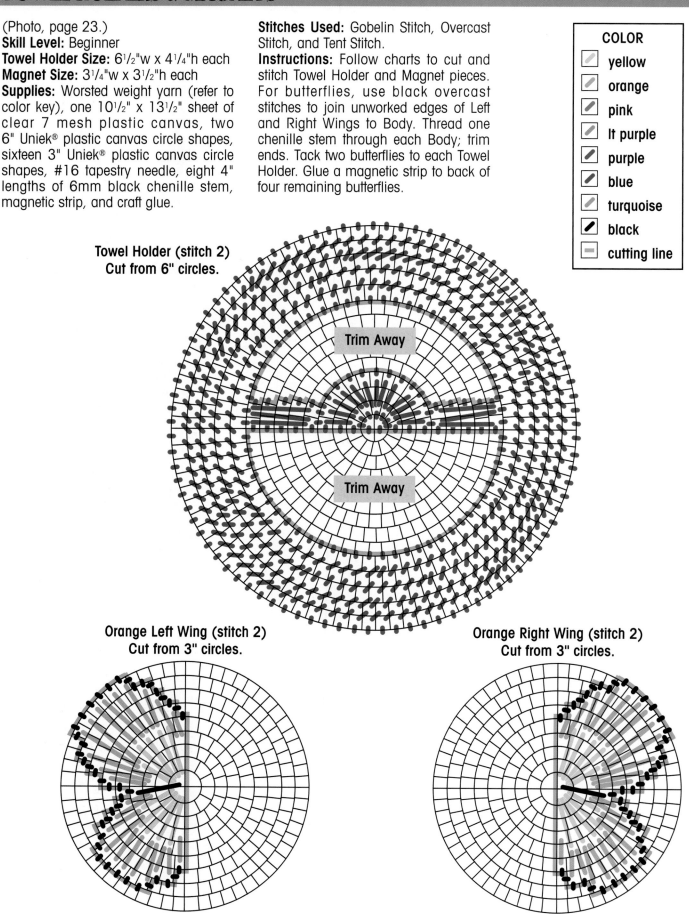

Towel Holder (stitch 2)
Cut from 6" circles.

Trim Away

Trim Away

Orange Left Wing (stitch 2)
Cut from 3" circles.

Orange Right Wing (stitch 2)
Cut from 3" circles.

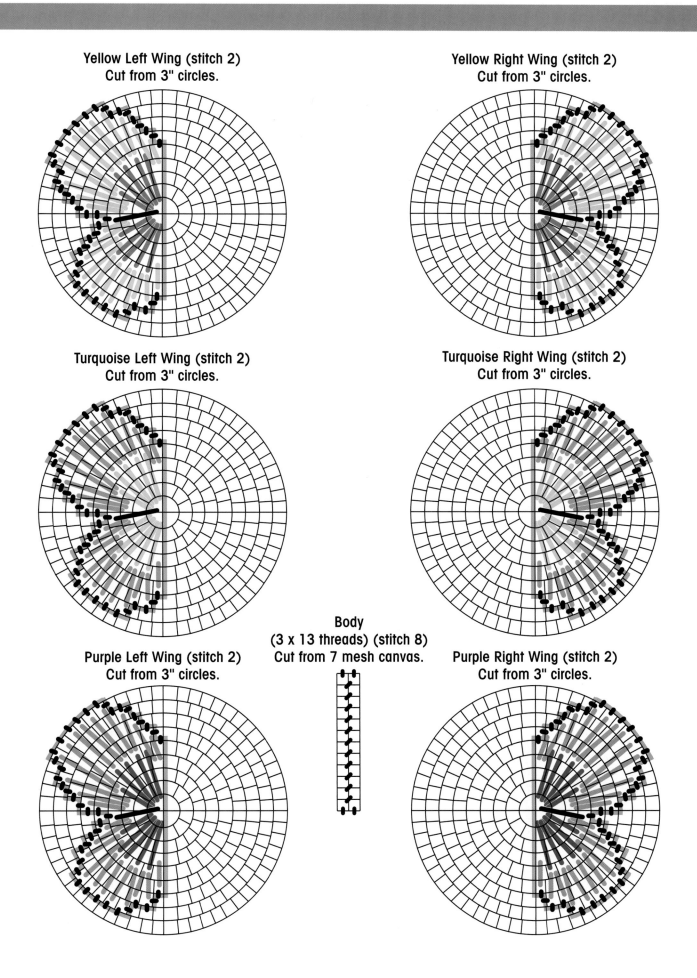

Yellow Left Wing (stitch 2)
Cut from 3" circles.

Yellow Right Wing (stitch 2)
Cut from 3" circles.

Turquoise Left Wing (stitch 2)
Cut from 3" circles.

Turquoise Right Wing (stitch 2)
Cut from 3" circles.

Purple Left Wing (stitch 2)
Cut from 3" circles.

Body
(3 x 13 threads) (stitch 8)
Cut from 7 mesh canvas.

Purple Right Wing (stitch 2)
Cut from 3" circles.

(Photo, page 22.)
Skill Level: Beginner
Size: 9"w x 7½"h each, excluding cord and ribbons
Supplies for one Windsock: Worsted weight yarn (refer to color key), six 6" Uniek® plastic canvas heart shapes, #16 tapestry needle, 18" length of cord, one 6" length of 6mm black chenille stem, eight 18" lengths of ¾"w ribbon, and craft glue.
Stitches Used: Gobelin Stitch, Overcast Stitch, and Tent Stitch.
Instructions: Follow charts to cut and stitch Purple or Blue Butterfly Windsock pieces. Matching ♥'s, use black overcast stitches to join Butterfly Wing Fronts; repeat for Backs. Thread cord ends through Front Wings at ■'s, and knot on back of Front Wings. With wrong sides together, join unworked edges of Front Wings to Back Wings. Thread chenille stem through Body Front; trim ends. Join Body Front to Body Back along unworked edges at bottom. Place Wings between Body Front and Back. Join remaining unworked edges at top of Body Front and Back. Glue ribbon ends between Wings at open edges; trim ends.

COLOR	
✎	white
✎	orange
✎	lt purple
✎	purple
✎	blue
✎	dk blue
✏	black
▬	cutting line

Body Front/Back
(stitch 2 for Purple Butterfly)
(stitch 2 for Blue Butterfly)
Cut from 6" hearts.

Purple Butterfly Front/Back Wing
(stitch 2 for Purple Butterfly)
Cut from 6" hearts.

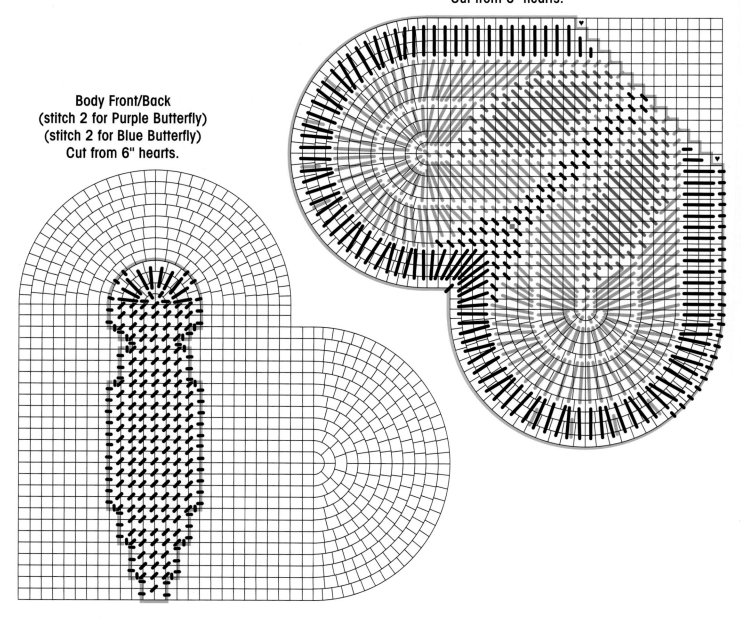

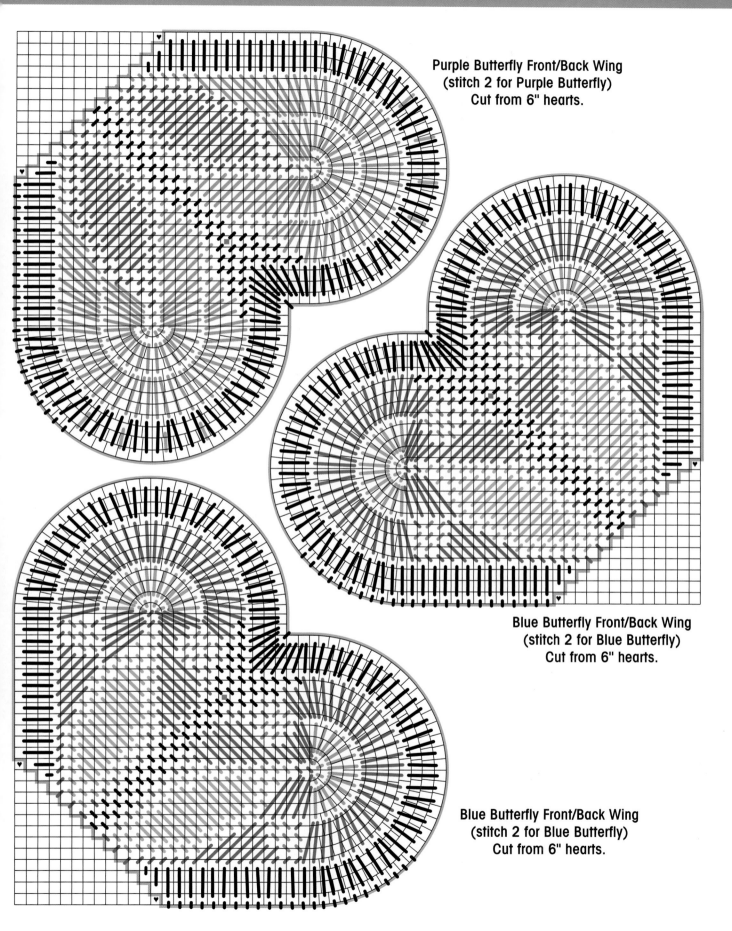

Purple Butterfly Front/Back Wing
(stitch 2 for Purple Butterfly)
Cut from 6" hearts.

Blue Butterfly Front/Back Wing
(stitch 2 for Blue Butterfly)
Cut from 6" hearts.

Blue Butterfly Front/Back Wing
(stitch 2 for Blue Butterfly)
Cut from 6" hearts.

Bug-Catcher's Box

Your young entomologist will definitely want to inspect this insect cage! Made from bright yellow mesh, the lightweight bug-catcher's box is ideal for real, live creepy-crawlers or as a cache for other natural treasures gathered during an outdoor expedition. Companion bee and ladybug magnets add to the fun!

Skill Level: Beginner

Cage Size: 5³/₄"w x 7³/₄"h x 3³/₄"d

Approx. Magnet Size: 2¹/₂"w x 3"h each

Supplies: Worsted weight yarn (refer to color keys), one 10¹/₂" x 13¹/₂" sheet of fluorescent yellow 7 mesh plastic canvas, five 6" Uniek® plastic canvas heart shapes, one 3" Uniek® plastic canvas circle shape, #16 tapestry needle, one ³/₄" paper fastener, three 3" lengths of 6mm black chenille stem, magnetic strip, and craft glue.

Stitches Used: Gobelin Stitch, Lazy Daisy Stitch, Overcast Stitch, and Tent Stitch.

Instructions: Follow charts to cut and stitch Bug Cage and Magnet pieces, working lazy daisy stitches last and leaving blue shaded areas on Cage unworked. Cut the following pieces from fluorescent yellow 7 mesh canvas:

End Bottom (7 x 25 threads) (cut 2)
End Side (7 x 87 threads) (cut 2)
Bottom (37 x 23 threads)
Handle (7 x 46 threads)

These pieces are not stitched. Referring to Diagram, use yellow overcast stitches to join long edges of Bottom to short edges of Cage. Work stitches in blue shaded areas to join short edges of Handle to Cage. Join End Side and End Bottom along short edges. Join End Bottom and End Sides to End. Repeat for Door End. Insert paper fastener in Door and Door End at ★. Secure fastener on back of Door End. Tack Wings to Ladybugs and Bee. Thread one chenille stem through each Ladybug and Bee; trim ends. Tack a Ladybug to Cage. Glue magnetic strips to back of remaining Ladybug and Bee.

COLOR	
⟋	yellow - 43 yds
⊟	cutting line

Door
Cut from 3" circle.
Use yellow overcast stitches to cover
unworked edges of Door.

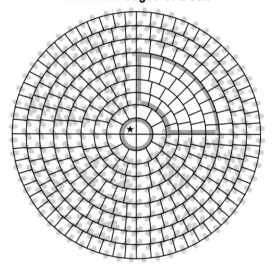

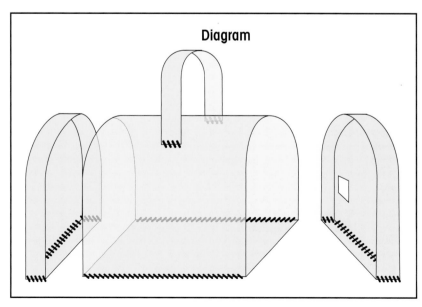

Diagram

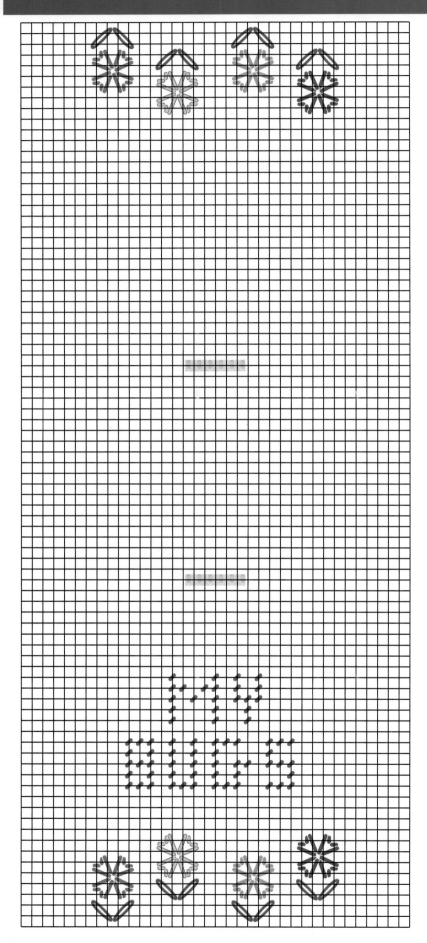

Cage (37 x 85 threads)
Cut from florescent yellow 7 mesh canvas.

COLOR	
⬜	yellow
⬜	orange - 1 yd
⬜	pink - 1 yd
⬜	purple - 1 yd
⬜	lt blue - 1 yd
⬜	blue - 2 yds
⬜	green lazy daisy - 2 yds
▬	cutting line

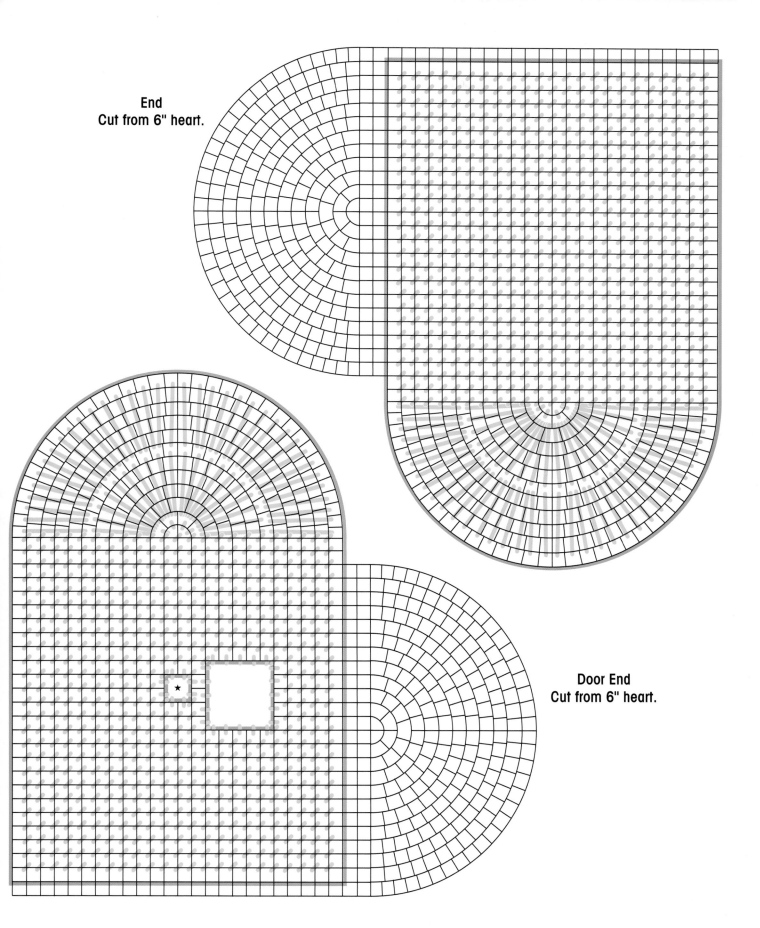

End
Cut from 6" heart.

Door End
Cut from 6" heart.

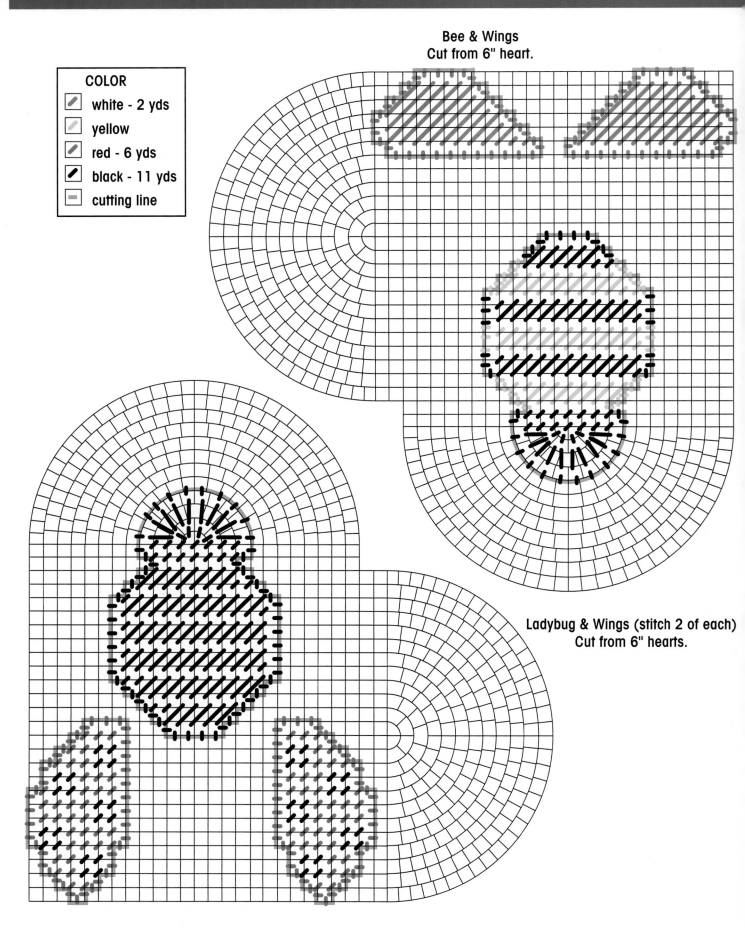

COLOR
- white - 2 yds
- yellow
- red - 6 yds
- black - 11 yds
- cutting line

Bee & Wings
Cut from 6" heart.

Ladybug & Wings (stitch 2 of each)
Cut from 6" hearts.

Puppy Love

Your little one will have her first case of "puppy love" when you stitch this fetching tissue topper!
The easy-to-care-for pup makes a great pal for Baby and a handy helper for Mom and Dad.

TISSUE BOX COVER

(Photo, page 33.)
Skill Level: Beginner
Size: 6¼"w x 9"h x 5¼"d
(Fits a 4¼"w x 5¼"h x 4¼"d boutique tissue box.)
Supplies: Worsted weight yarn (refer to color keys), two 10½" x 13½" sheets of clear 7 mesh plastic canvas, three 6" Uniek® plastic canvas heart shapes, two 3" Uniek® plastic canvas circle shapes, and #16 tapestry needle.
Stitches Used: Backstitch, Gobelin Stitch, Overcast Stitch, and Tent Stitch.
Instructions: Follow charts to cut and stitch Tissue Box Cover pieces, working backstitches last and leaving pink shaded area unworked. Matching ♥'s and ★'s, work stitches in pink shaded

area to join Top to Tail Front. Using brown overcast stitches, join Tail Front to Back. Matching ✖'s and ▲'s and working through three layers of canvas, join unworked edge of Left Leg to Side and Back. Matching ■'s and ◆'s and working through three layers of canvas, join unworked edge of Right Leg to Side and Back. Join remaining unworked edges of Sides to Back. Tack Legs to Sides. Join Front to Sides. Join Top to Front, Sides, and remaining unworked edges of Back. Tack Paws to Front. With wrong sides together, use dk brown overcast stitches to join Ears Front to Ears Back. Tack Head to Ears; tack Head and Ears to Front.

COLOR	
✎	white - 1 yd
✎	cream - 4 yds
✎	lt pink - 1 yd
✎	pink - 1 yd
✎	blue - 1 yd
✎	lt brown - 82 yds
✎	brown - 18 yds
✦	black - 2 yds
✎	*black
▬	cutting line

*Use 2 plies of yarn.

Top (31 x 31 threads)
Cut from 7 mesh canvas.

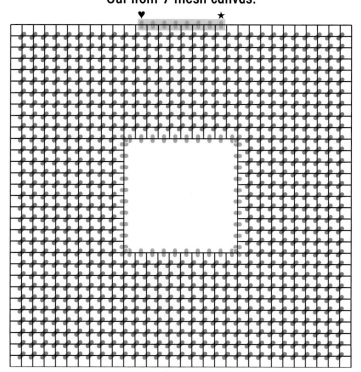

Front/Side (31 x 38 threads) (stitch 3)
Cut from 7 mesh canvas.

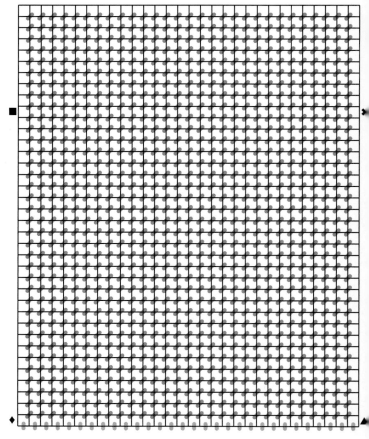

Head
Cut from 6" heart.

Back (31 x 59 threads)
Cut from 7 mesh canvas.

Tail Front (17 x 22 threads)
Cut from 7 mesh canvas.

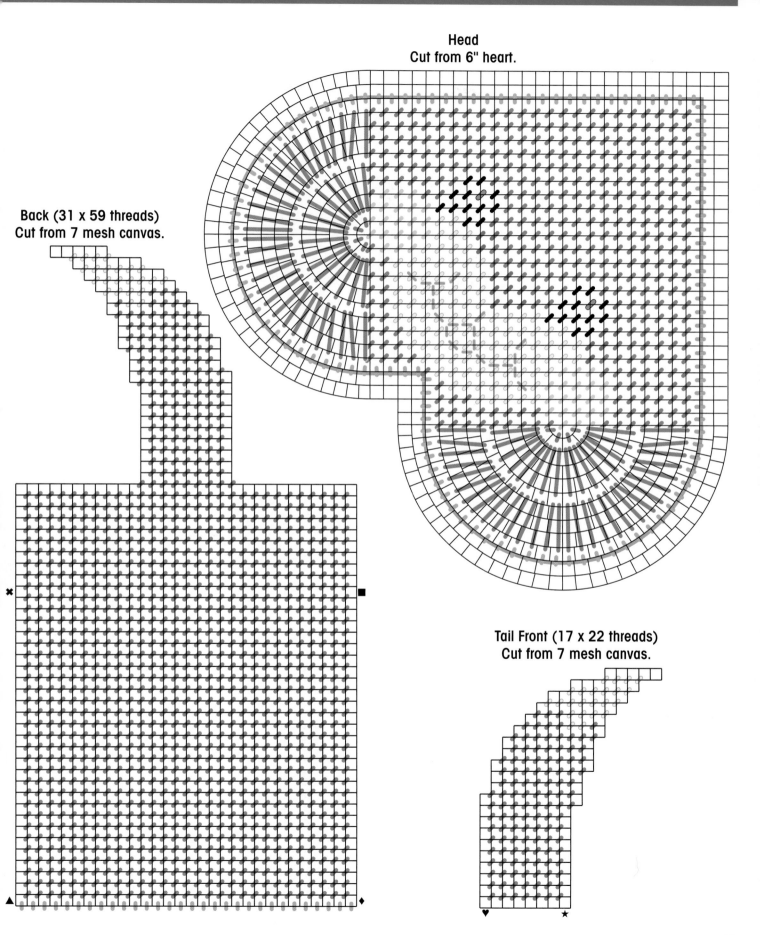

Ears Front/Back (stitch 2)
Cut from 6" hearts.

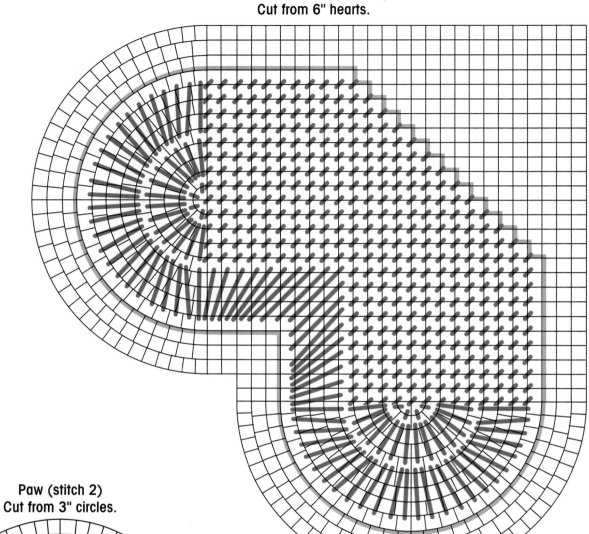

Paw (stitch 2)
Cut from 3" circles.

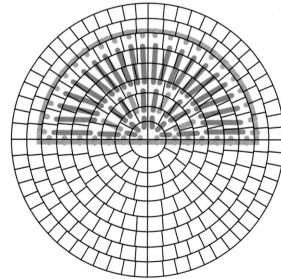

Right Leg (31 x 31 threads)
Cut from 7 mesh canvas.

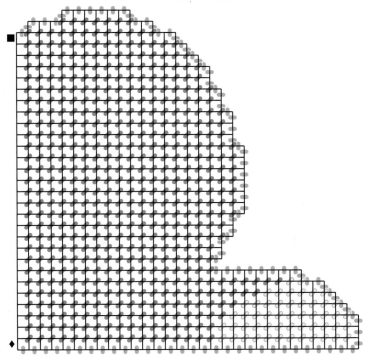

COLOR	
⊘	cream
⊘	lt brown
⊘	brown
⊘	dk brown - 31 yds
⊟	cutting line

Left Leg (31 x 31 threads)
Cut from 7 mesh canvas.

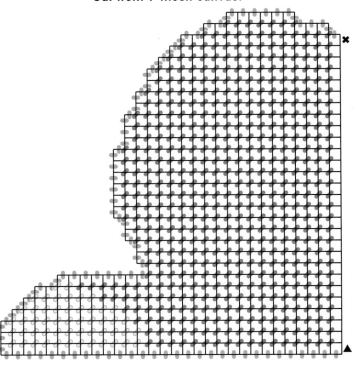

Kitten Caboodle

For the feline lover in your life, this kitten caboodle will be the cat's meow! Perk up her room with a tissue topper, a scissor holder, and a "purr-fect" picture frame. She'll have no problem keeping up with her hair barrettes when she hangs them on the tail of this friendly tabby.

(Photo, page 38.)

Skill Level: Beginner

Size: 6¼"w x 9½"h x 5¼"d

(Fits a 4¼"w x 5¼"h x 4¼"d boutique tissue box.)

Supplies: Worsted weight yarn (refer to color key), two 10½" x 13½" sheets of clear 7 mesh plastic canvas, two 6" Uniek® plastic canvas heart shapes, two 3" Uniek® plastic canvas circle shapes, one 5" Uniek® plastic canvas hexagon shape, and #16 tapestry needle.

Stitches Used: Backstitch, Gobelin Stitch, Overcast Stitch, and Tent Stitch.

Instructions: Follow charts to cut and stitch Tissue Box Cover pieces, working backstitches last and leaving pink shaded area unworked. Matching ♥'s and ★'s, work stitches in pink shaded area to join Top to Tail Front. Referring to photo for yarn colors, use overcast stitches to join Tail Front to Back. Matching ■'s and ▲'s and working through three layers of canvas, use dk grey overcast stitches to join unworked edge of Left Leg to Side and Back. Matching ♦'s and ♣'s and working through three layers of canvas, join unworked edge of Right Leg to Side and Back. Join remaining unworked edges of Sides to Back. Tack Legs to Sides. Join Front to Sides. Join Top to Front, Sides, and remaining unworked edges of Back. Matching ✖'s and ♠'s, join Ear Fronts to Head Front and Ear Backs to Head Back. Join Head Front to Head Back. Tack Paws and Head to Front.

COLOR	
⬜	white
⬜	lt pink
⬜	pink
⬜	blue
⬜	grey
⬛	dk grey
⬜	black
⬜	*black
⬜	cutting line

*Use 2 plies of yarn.

Top (31 x 31 threads)
Cut from 7 mesh canvas.

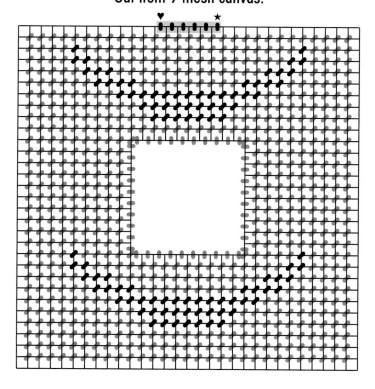

Front/Side (31 x 38 threads) (stitch 3)
Cut from 7 mesh canvas.

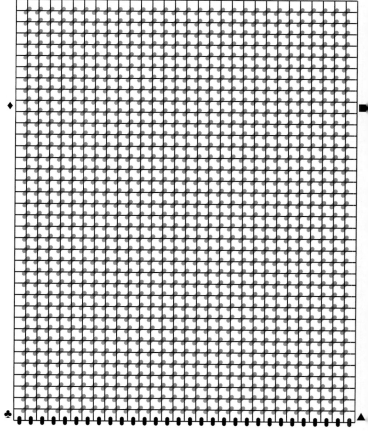

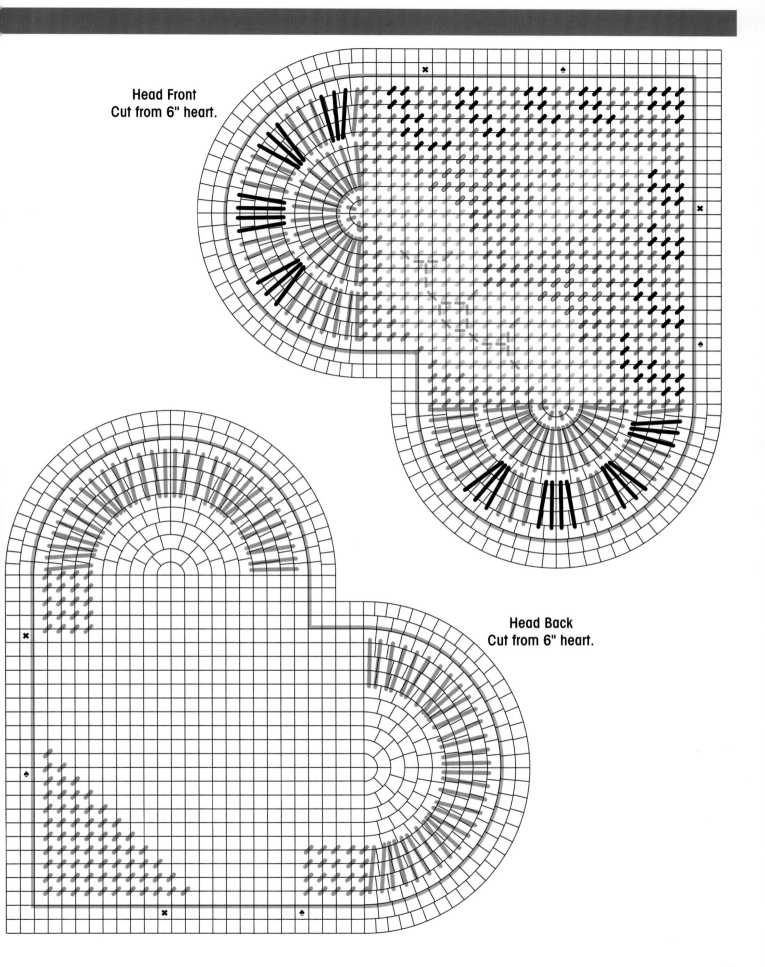

Head Front
Cut from 6" heart.

Head Back
Cut from 6" heart.

Paw (stitch 2)
Cut from 3" circles.

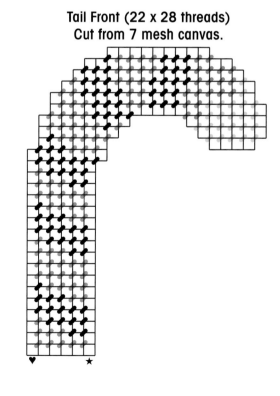

Back (34 x 65 threads)
Cut from 7 mesh canvas.

Tail Front (22 x 28 threads)
Cut from 7 mesh canvas.

Ear Front/Backs
Cut from 5" hexagon.

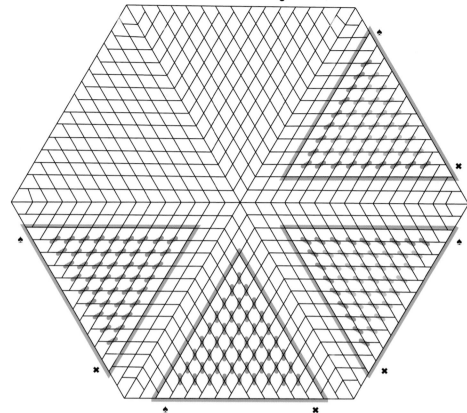

COLOR	
⟋	white
⟋	lt pink
⟋	grey
✎	dk grey
▬	cutting line

Left Leg (31 x 31 threads)
Cut from 7 mesh canvas.

Right Leg (31 x 31 threads)
Cut from 7 mesh canvas.

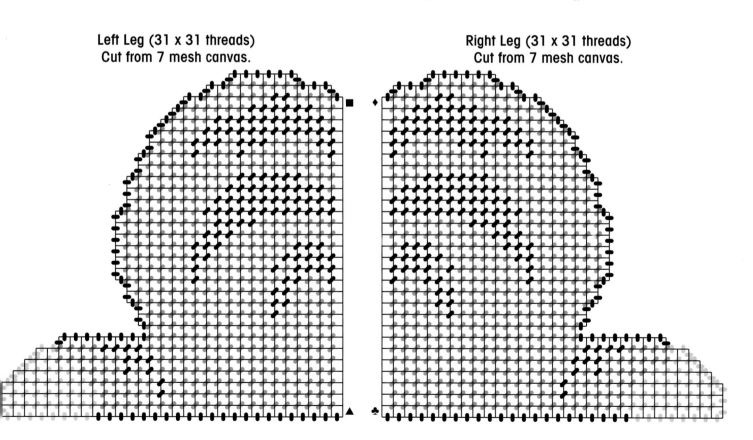

(Photo, page 39.)
Skill Level: Beginner
Size: 7³/₄"w x 7¹/₂"h
(Photo opening is 3¹/₄"w x 2³/₄"h.)
Supplies: Worsted weight yarn (refer to color key), one 10¹/₂" x 13¹/₂" sheet of clear 7 mesh plastic canvas, three 6" Uniek® plastic canvas heart shapes, three 3" Darice® plastic canvas heart shapes, one 5" Uniek® plastic canvas hexagon shape, and #16 tapestry needle.
Stitches Used: Backstitch, Gobelin Stitch, Overcast Stitch, and Tent Stitch.

Instructions: Follow charts to cut and stitch Frame pieces, working backstitches last. Matching ♥'s and ★'s, use dk grey overcast stitches to join Ear Fronts to Head Front and Ear Backs to Head Back. Join Head Front to Head Back. Tack Head and Paws to Front. Join Stand Front to Stand Back. Referring to Diagram, tack Stand to Back. For Tail, match ✖'s and ♦'s and join Tail Front to Front and Tail Back to Back. Join remaining unworked edges of Front and Back.

COLOR	
⬜	white
⬜	lt pink
⬜	pink
⬜	blue
⬜	grey
⬛	dk grey
⬜	black
⬜	*black
⊟	cutting line

*Use 2 plies of yarn.

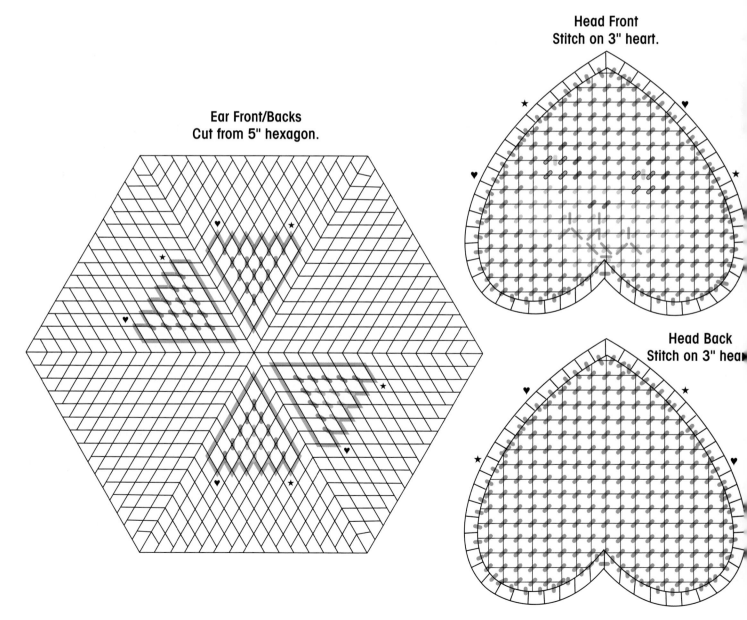

Ear Front/Backs
Cut from 5" hexagon.

Head Front
Stitch on 3" heart.

Head Back
Stitch on 3" heart.

Paws
Cut from 6" heart.

Tail Front/Back
Cut from 6" heart.

Diagram

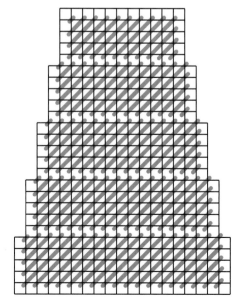

Back

Stand

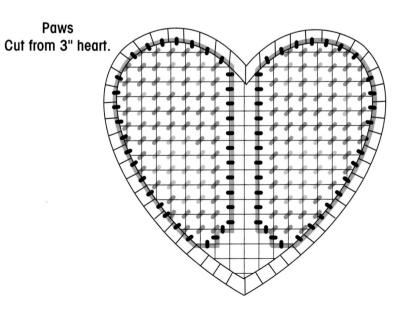

Stand Front/Back
(20 x 26 threads) (cut 2) (stitch 1)
Cut from 7 mesh canvas.

Paws
Cut from 3" heart.

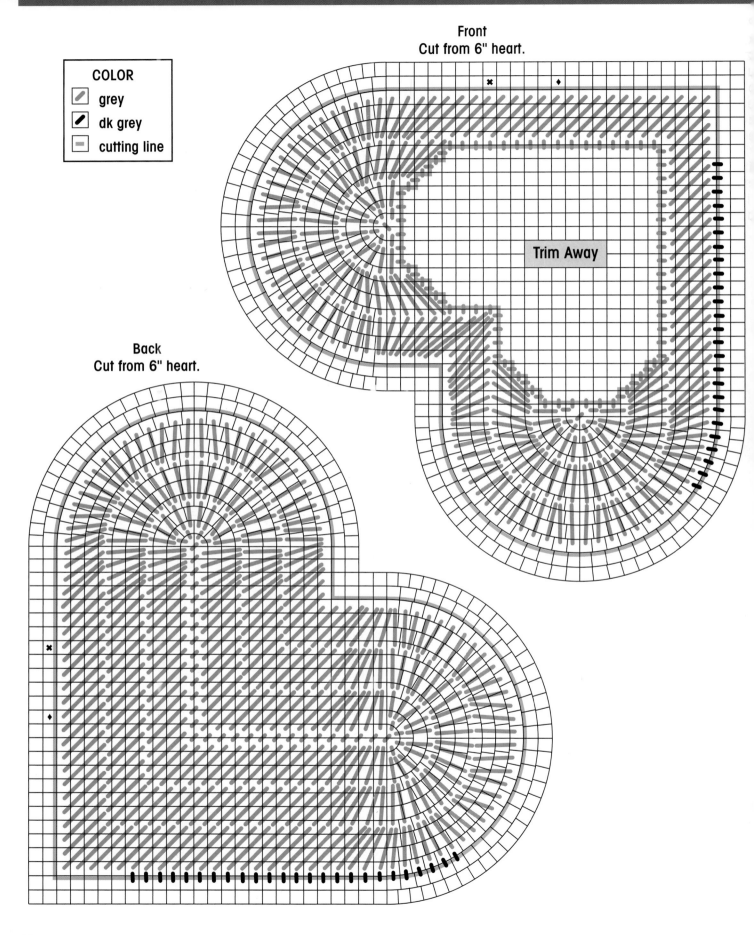

Front
Cut from 6" heart.

COLOR
grey
dk grey
cutting line

Trim Away

Back
Cut from 6" heart.

(Photo, page 39.)

Skill Level: Beginner

Size: 7¹⁄₄"w x 21¹⁄₂"h

Supplies: Worsted weight yarn (refer to color key), five 6" Uniek® plastic canvas heart shapes, one 5" Uniek® plastic canvas hexagon shape, #16 tapestry needle, and one sawtooth hanger.

Stitches Used: Backstitch, Gobelin Stitch, Overcast Stitch, and Tent Stitch.

Instructions: Follow charts to cut and stitch Clipper pieces, working backstitches last. Matching ♥'s and ★'s, use dk grey overcast stitches to join Ear Fronts to Head Front and Ear Backs to Head Back. Join unworked edges of Head Front to Head Back. Matching ✖'s and ▲'s, join Paws to Body Front and Body Back. Join remaining unworked edges of Body Front to Body Back. Tack Body between open edges of Head Front and Head Back. For Tail, cut nine 1yd lengths of grey yarn. Fold in half and tie at fold. Braid Tail and tie end. Tack Tail to Back.

COLOR	
⟋	lt pink
⟋	grey
−	cutting line

Ear Front/Backs
Cut from 5" hexagon.

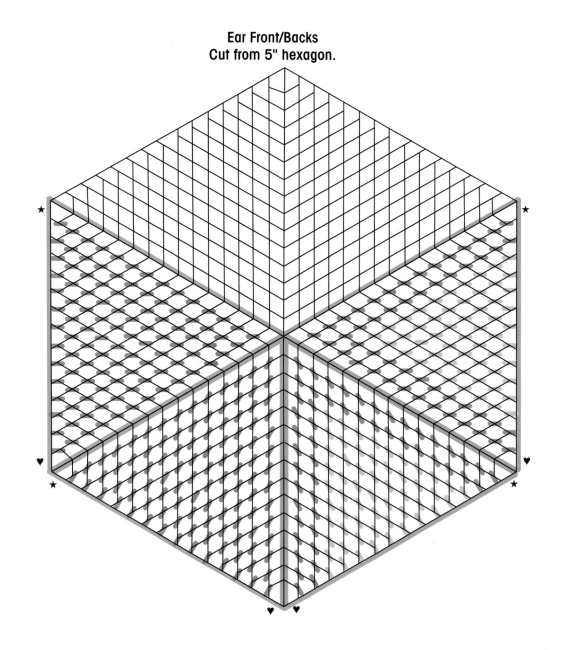

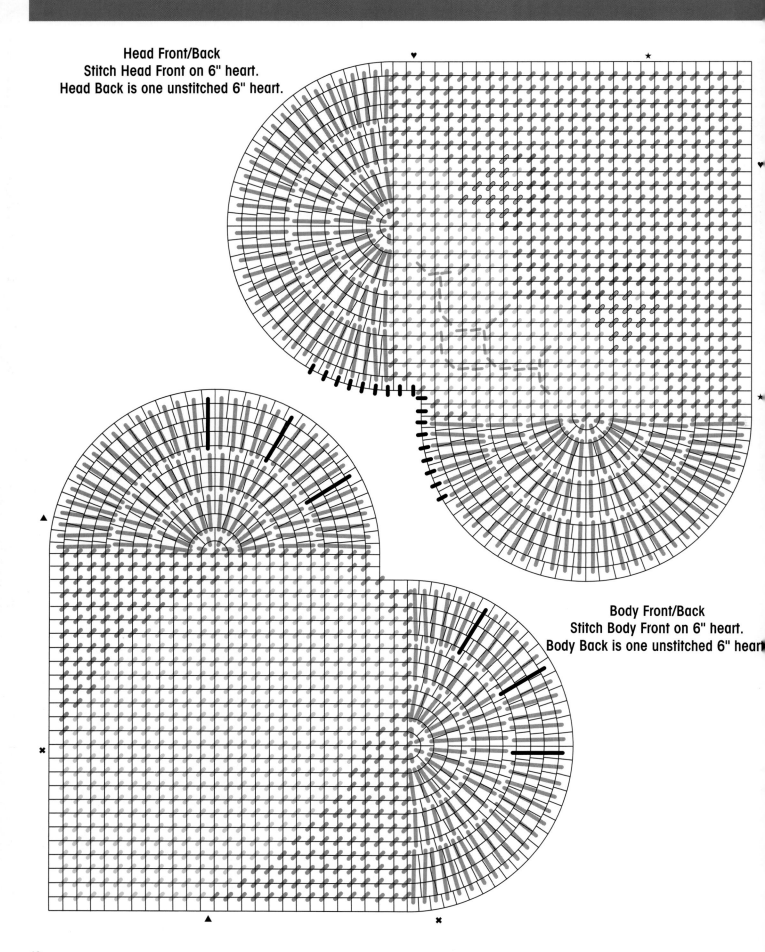

Head Front/Back
Stitch Head Front on 6" heart.
Head Back is one unstitched 6" heart.

Body Front/Back
Stitch Body Front on 6" heart.
Body Back is one unstitched 6" heart

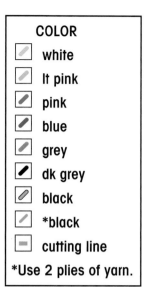

COLOR

white
lt pink
pink
blue
grey
dk grey
black
*black
cutting line

*Use 2 plies of yarn.

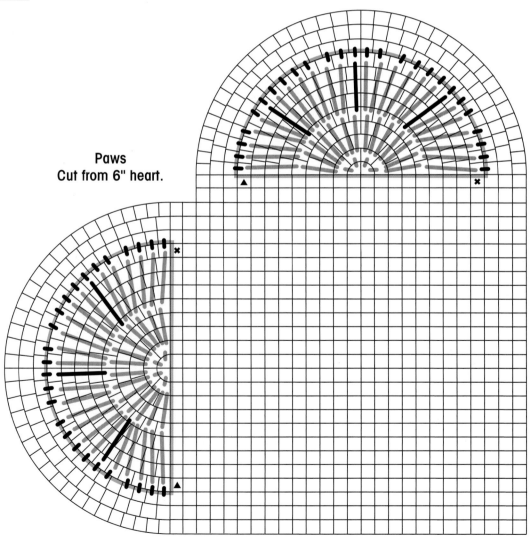

Paws
Cut from 6" heart.

SCISSOR HOLDER

(Photo, page 39.)

Skill Level: Beginner

Size: 3½"w x 6¾"h

Supplies: Worsted weight yarn (refer to color key), three 6" Uniek® plastic canvas heart shapes, two 3" Darice® plastic canvas heart shapes, one 5" Uniek® plastic canvas hexagon shape, and #16 tapestry needle.

Stitches Used: Backstitch, Gobelin Stitch, Overcast Stitch, and Tent Stitch.

Instructions: Follow charts to cut and stitch Scissor Holder pieces, working backstitches last. With wrong sides together, stack Holder Front and Holder Back. Matching ♦'s and ✖'s, use dk grey overcast stitches to join Pocket to Holder Front and Holder Back, working through three layers of canvas. Join remaining unworked edges of Holder Front and Holder Back. Tack Holder to wrong side of Head Back. Matching ♥'s and ★'s, join Ear Fronts to Head Front and Ear Backs to Head Back. Join Head Front to Head Back.

COLOR	
⟋	white
⟋	lt pink
⟋	pink
⟋	blue
⟋	grey
✎	dk grey
⟋	black
⟋	*black
▭	cutting line

*Use 2 plies of yarn.

Head Front
Stitch on 3" heart.

Head Back
Stitch on 3" heart.

Ear Front/Backs
Cut from 5" hexagon.

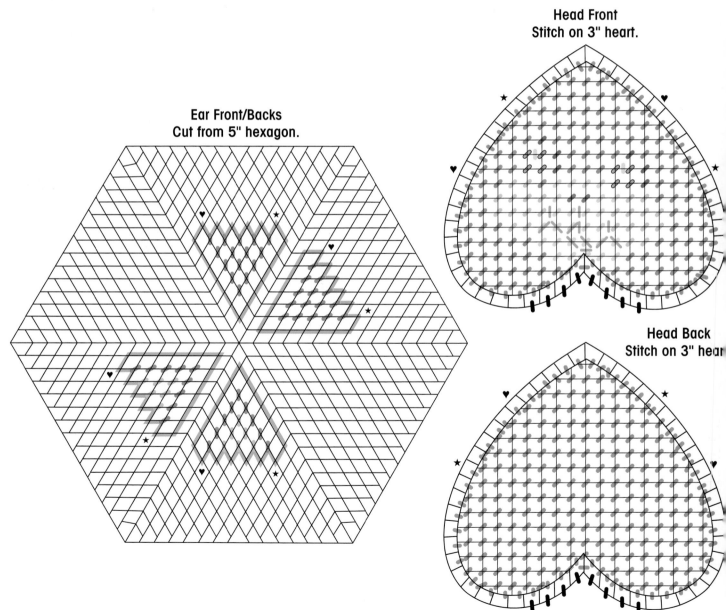

50

Holder Front/Back (stitch 2)
Cut from 6" hearts.

Pocket
Cut from 6" heart.

"Cub" House Companions

Jazz up your child's "cub" house with a wonderful wall hanging. Girls will love a heart balloon-toting teddy and a sweet photo frame. Boys will appreciate the "all star" baseball bear and handy scissor holder.

FRAME

(Photo, page 52.)
Skill Level: Beginner
Size: 6"w x 7¼"h
(Photo opening is 3¼"w x 2¾"h.)
Supplies: Worsted weight yarn (refer to color key), one 10½" x 13½" sheet of clear 7 mesh plastic canvas, three 6" Uniek® plastic canvas heart shapes, three 3" Darice® plastic canvas heart shapes, and #16 tapestry needle.
Stitches Used: Backstitch, Gobelin Stitch, Overcast Stitch, and Tent Stitch.

Instructions: Follow charts to cut and stitch Frame pieces, working backstitches last. Matching ♥'s and ★'s, use brown overcast stitches to join Ear Fronts to Head Front and Ear Backs to Head Back. Join Head Front to Head Back. Tack Head and Paws to Front. Join Stand Front to Stand Back. Referring to Diagram, tack Stand to Back. With wrong sides together, join Front and Back along unworked edges.

Stand Front/Back
(20 x 26 threads) (cut 2) (stitch 1)
Cut from 7 mesh canvas.

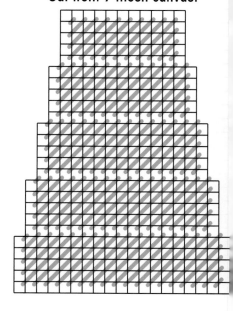

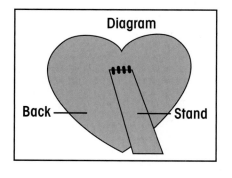

Diagram

Back — — Stand

COLOR	
✎	white
✎	cream
✎	lt pink
✎	blue
✎	lt brown
✎	brown
✎	black
✎	*black
—	cutting line
*Use 2 plies of yarn.	

Head Front
Stitch on 3" heart.

Head Back
Stitch on 3" heart.

Paws
Cut from 3" heart.

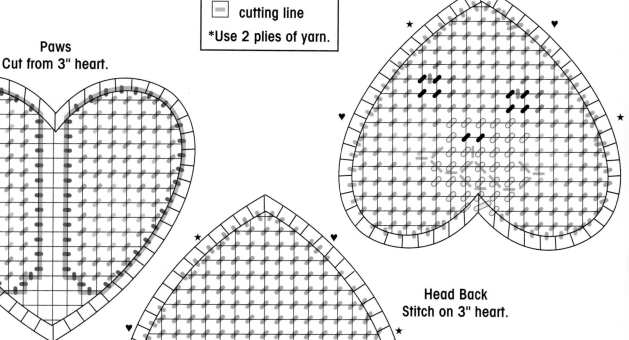

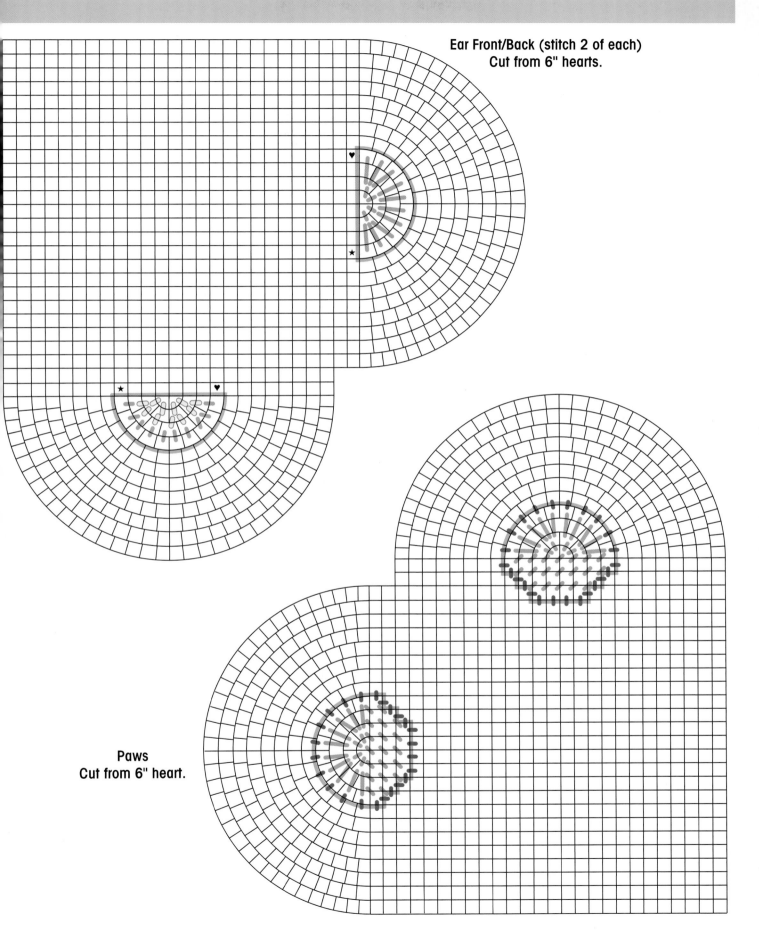

Ear Front/Back (stitch 2 of each)
Cut from 6" hearts.

Paws
Cut from 6" heart.

Front
Cut from 6" heart.

COLOR
- lt brown
- brown
- cutting line

Trim Away

Back
Cut from 6" heart.

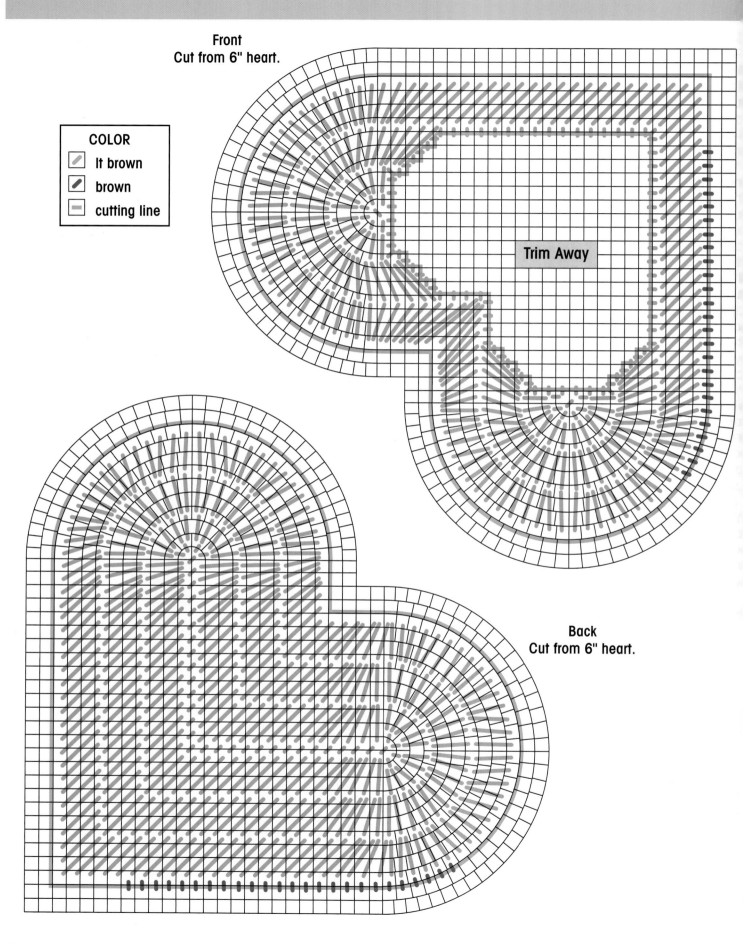

GIRL TEDDY

(Photo, page 52.)

Skill Level: Beginner

Size: 11³/₄"w x 15"h

Supplies: Worsted weight yarn (refer to color keys), one 10¹/₂" x 13¹/₂" sheet of clear 7 mesh plastic canvas, four 6" Uniek® plastic canvas heart shapes, two 4" Uniek® plastic canvas circle shapes, one 5" Uniek® plastic canvas hexagon shape, #16 tapestry needle, one 6" length of ¹/₄"w pink ribbon, two 4" lengths of ¹/₄"w pink ribbon, one sawtooth hanger, and craft glue.

Stitches Used: Backstitch, Gobelin Stitch, Overcast Stitch, and Tent Stitch.

Instructions: Follow charts to cut and stitch Girl Wall Hanging pieces, working backstitches last and leaving green shaded area unworked. Using brown overcast stitches, join Ears to unworked edges of Head. Matching ♥'s and ★'s, work stitches in green shaded area to join unworked edge of Paw to Left Arm. Join unworked edge of Left Arm to unworked edge of Body. Tack Head to Body. Tack Bow pieces together at ✖'s. Tack Knot to Bow. Tack Bow to Head. Tack Balloons together and to back of Head and Ear. Thread 4" ribbons through Purple Balloon and glue to back of Balloon. Placing ribbons under Paw, glue ribbons to Left Arm; tack Paw in place. Tie bow with 6" ribbon. Glue Bow to Left Arm; trim ribbon ends. Tack Right Arm and Feet to Body. Securely tack hanger to back of Balloons.

BOY TEDDY

(Photo, page 53.)

Skill Level: Beginner

Size: 11³/₄"w x 15"h

Supplies: Worsted weight yarn (refer to color keys), one 10¹/₂" x 13¹/₂" sheet of clear 7 mesh plastic canvas, two 6" Uniek® plastic canvas heart shapes, two 4" Uniek® plastic canvas circle shapes, four 3" Uniek® plastic canvas circle shapes, three 5" Uniek® plastic canvas star shapes, #16 tapestry needle, and one sawtooth hanger.

Stitches Used: Backstitch, Gobelin Stitch, Overcast Stitch, and Tent Stitch.

Instructions: Follow charts to cut and stitch Boy Wall Hanging pieces, working backstitches last and leaving green shaded area unworked. Using brown overcast stitches, join Ears to unworked edges of Head. Matching ♥'s and ★'s, work stitches in green shaded area to join unworked edge of Paw to Left Arm. Join unworked edge of Left Arm to unworked edge of Body. Tack Head to Body. With right sides together, use dk blue overcast stitches to join Bill to unworked edge of Cap. Tack Pompom to Cap. Tack Cap to Head. Tack Stars together and to back of Ears. Tack #1 to center Star. Tack Bat to Star and under Paw. Tack Ball to back of Right Arm; tack Right Arm and Feet to Body. Securely tack hanger to back of center Star.

Girl/Boy Left Foot
(16 x 17 threads)
Cut from 7 mesh canvas.

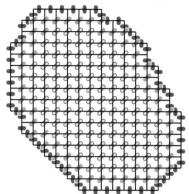

Girl/Boy Right Foot
(16 x 17 threads)
Cut from 7 mesh canvas.

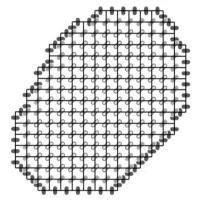

COLOR	
⟋	cream
⟋	lt brown
⟋	brown

Girl/Boy Right Arm
(17 x 22 threads)
Cut from 7 mesh canvas.

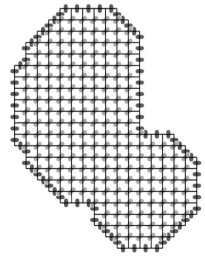

Girl/Boy Left Arm
(23 x 22 threads)
Cut from 7 mesh canvas.

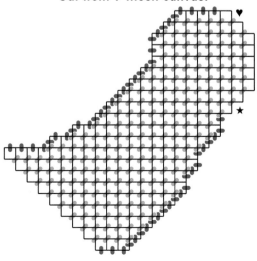

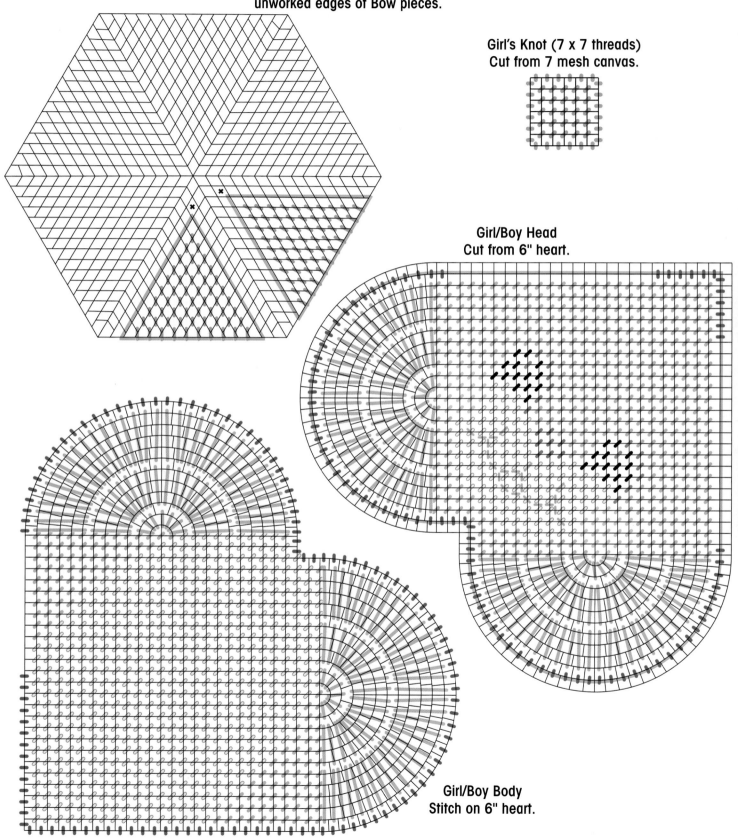

Girl's Bow
Cut from 5" hexagon.
Use lavender overcast stitches to cover
unworked edges of Bow pieces.

Girl's Knot (7 x 7 threads)
Cut from 7 mesh canvas.

Girl/Boy Head
Cut from 6" heart.

Girl/Boy Body
Stitch on 6" heart.

COLOR

- ⬚ white
- ⬚ cream
- ⬚ lt pink
- ⬚ pink
- ⬚ lavender
- ⬚ purple
- ⬚ blue
- ⬚ lt brown
- ⬚ brown
- ⬛ black
- ⬚ *white
- ⬚ *black
- ▬ cutting line

Girl/Boy Ear (stitch 2)
Cut from 3" circles.

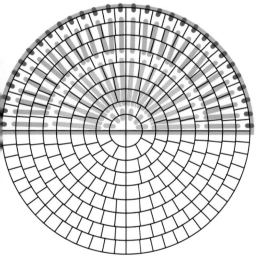

Girl/Boy Paw
(10 x 10 threads)
Cut from 7 mesh canvas.

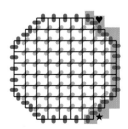

Girl's Pink Balloon
Stitch on 6" heart.

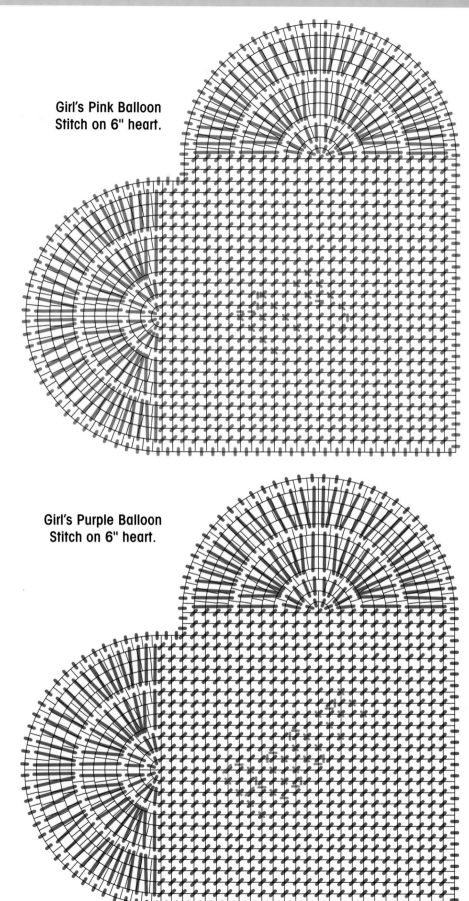

Girl's Purple Balloon
Stitch on 6" heart.

Boy's Bat (13 x 56 threads)
Cut from 7 mesh canvas.

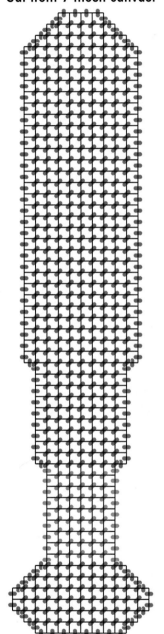

Boy's Cap
Cut from 4" circle.

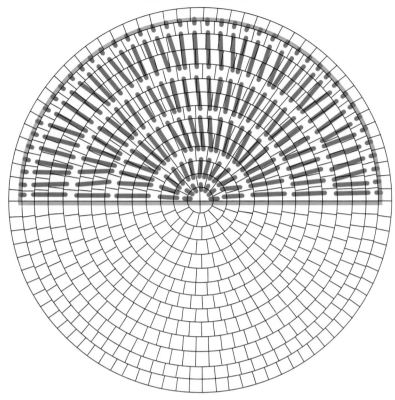

Boy's Bill
Cut from 4" circle.

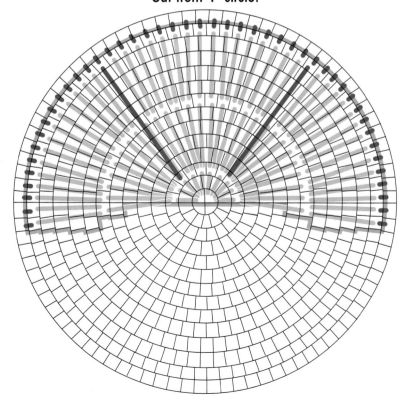

COLOR

- ✎ white
- ✎ red
- ✎ blue
- ✎ dk blue
- ✎ brown
- ✎ Star color
- ▬ cutting line

Boy's Ball
Cut from 3" circle.
Use white overcast stitches to cover
unworked edges of Ball.

Boy's Pom-pom
Cut from 3" circle.
Use white overcast stitches to cover
unworked edges of Pom-pom.

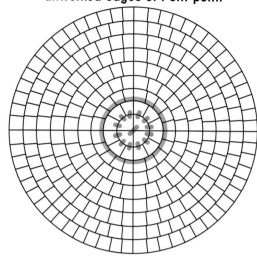

Boy's 1 (7 x 11 threads)
Cut from 7 mesh canvas.

Star
Stitch on 5" stars.
Stitch 1 red, 1 white, and 1 blue.

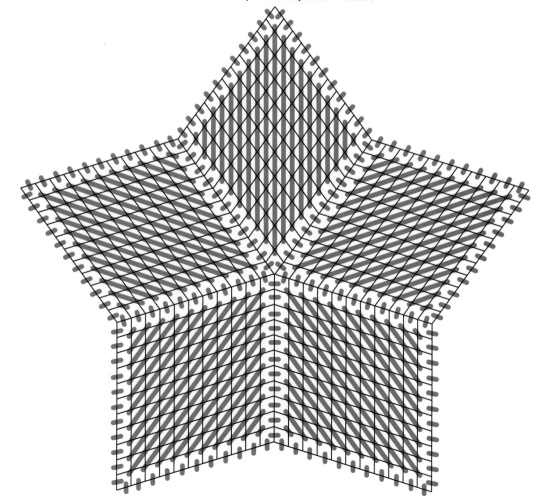

Boy's # (9 x 9 threads)
Cut from 7 mesh canvas.

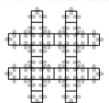

SCISSOR HOLDER

(Photo, page 53.)
Skill Level: Beginner
Size: 3¼"w x 6¾"h
Supplies: Worsted weight yarn (refer to color key), four 6" Uniek® plastic canvas heart shapes, two 3" Darice® plastic canvas heart shapes, and #16 tapestry needle.
Stitches Used: Backstitch, Gobelin Stitch, Overcast Stitch, and Tent Stitch.
Instructions: Follow charts to cut and stitch Scissor Holder pieces, working backstitches last. With wrong sides together, Stack Holder Front and Holder Back. Matching ♦'s and ✖'s, use brown overcast stitches to join Pocket to Holder Front and Holder Back, working through three layers of canvas. Join remaining unworked edges of Holder Front and Holder Back. Tack Holder to wrong side of Head Back. Matching ♥'s and ★'s, join Ear Fronts to Head Front and Ear Backs to Head Back. Join Head Front to Head Back.

COLOR	
▨	white
▨	cream
▨	lt pink
▨	blue
▨	lt brown
▨	brown
▨	black
▨	*black
▬	cutting line
*Use 2 plies of yarn.	

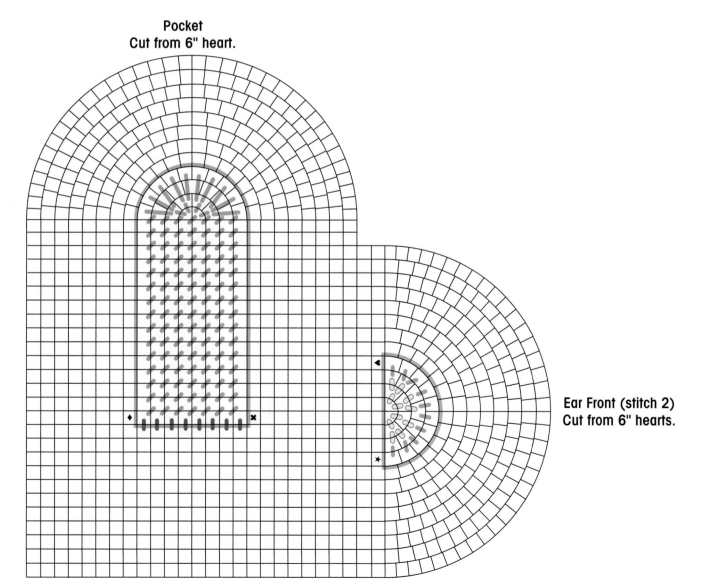

Pocket
Cut from 6" heart.

Ear Front (stitch 2)
Cut from 6" hearts.

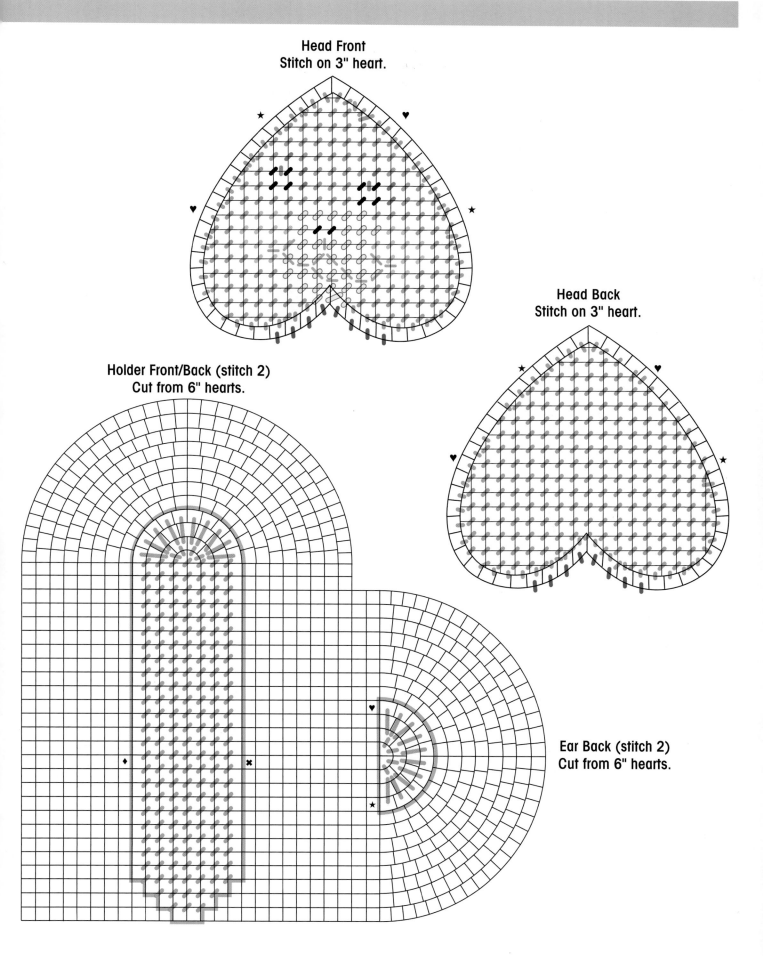

Head Front
Stitch on 3" heart.

Head Back
Stitch on 3" heart.

Holder Front/Back (stitch 2)
Cut from 6" hearts.

Ear Back (stitch 2)
Cut from 6" hearts.

Sporty Set

Score big with your young athlete by stitching up this sporty accessory set. Soccer, basketball, baseball, and football motifs highlight a treasure chest that's a real winner for storing trading cards or other sports paraphernalia. Fans will have a ball posting photos and game reminders with these catchy magnets. And the coasters are in a league of their own when it comes to keeping water rings off the furniture.

COASTER SET

(Photo, page 65.)

Skill Level: Beginner

Coaster Size: 4"w x 4"h each

Holder Size: 4¹/₂"w x 1¹/₂"h x 2"d

Supplies: Worsted weight yarn (refer to color key), eight 4" Uniek® plastic canvas square shapes or two 10¹/₂" x 13¹/₂" sheets of clear 7 mesh plastic canvas, one 10¹/₂" x 13¹/₂" sheet of clear 7 mesh plastic canvas, and #16 tapestry needle.

Stitches Used: Backstitch, Overcast Stitch, and Tent Stitch.

Instructions: Follow charts to cut and stitch Coaster Set pieces, working backstitches last. For Bottom, cut a piece of 7 mesh canvas 30 x 13 threads. Bottom is not worked. Using lt blue overcast stitches, join Front and Back to Sides along short edges. Join Bottom to Front, Back, and Sides.

COLOR	
✎	white - 17 yds
✎	orange - 7 yds
✎	red - 2 yds
✎	lt blue - 64 yds
✎	dk blue - 15 yds
✎	green - 32 yds
✎	lt brown - 3 yds
✎	black - 2 yds
✎	*white
✎	*brown - 1 yd

*Use 2 plies of yarn.

Front (30 x 11 threads)
Cut from 7 mesh canvas.

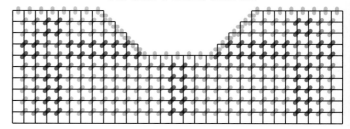

Side (13 x 11 threads) (stitch 2)
Cut from 7 mesh canvas.

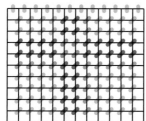

Back (30 x 11 threads)
Cut from 7 mesh canvas.

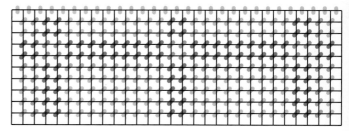

Basketball Coaster
(28 x 28 threads) (stitch 2)
Stitch on 4" squares or 7 mesh canvas.

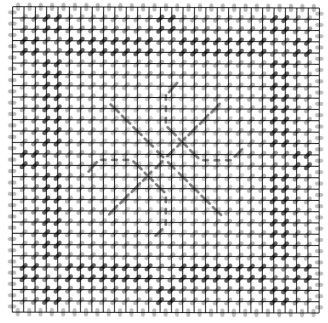

Baseball Coaster
(28 x 28 threads) (stitch 2)
Stitch on 4" squares or 7 mesh canvas.

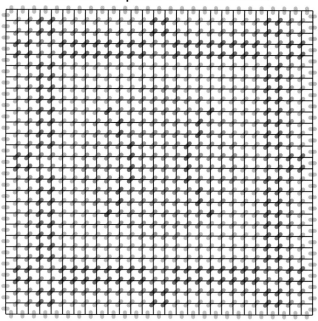

Football Coaster
(28 x 28 threads) (stitch 2)
Stitch on 4" squares or 7 mesh canvas.

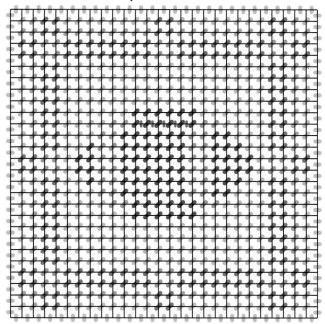

Soccer Coaster
(28 x 28 threads) (stitch 2)
Stitch on 4" squares or 7 mesh canvas.

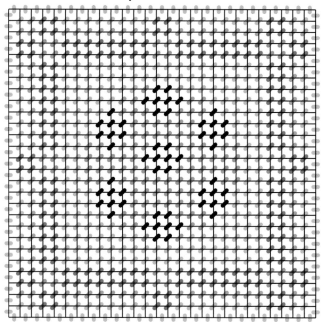

(Photo, page 64.)

Skill Level: Intermediate

Size: 6½"w x 5¾"h x 3¾"d

Supplies: Worsted weight yarn (refer to color key), four 6" Uniek® plastic canvas heart shapes, two 10½" x 13½" sheets of clear 7 mesh plastic canvas, #16 tapestry needle, and craft glue.

Stitches Used: Backstitch, Gobelin Stitch, Overcast Stitch, and Tent Stitch.

Instructions: Follow charts to cut and stitch Treasure Chest pieces, working backstitches last. Matching ▲'s and ■'s, use lt blue overcast stitches to join Lid Sides to Lid. Join one Inner Support to Lid Sides and front unworked edge of Lid. Join Box Sides to Box Front and Back along short edges. Join Bottom to Box Front, Back, and Sides. Join remaining Inner Support to Box Front and Sides. Join Lid to Box along unworked edges, stitching through all four layers of canvas. Tack Handles to Box Sides and Latch to Box Front.

COLOR	
✎	white - 7 yds
✎	orange - 2 yds
✎	red - 1 yd
✎	lt blue - 71 yds
✎	dk blue - 15 yds
✎	green - 14 yds
✎	lt brown - 2 yds
✎	black - 1 yd
✎	*white
✎	*brown - 1 yd
*Use 2 plies of yarn.	

Bottom (42 x 25 threads)
Cut from 7 mesh canvas.

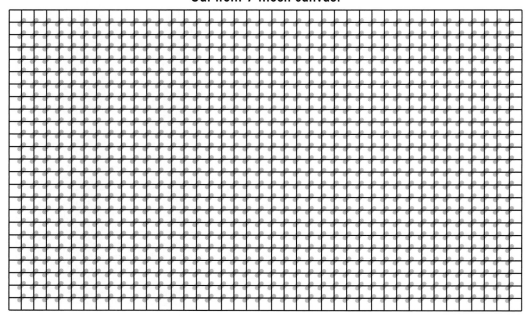

Box Front/Back
(42 x 22 threads) (stitch 2)
Cut from 7 mesh canvas.

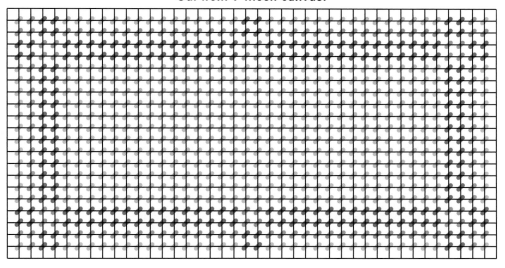

Lid (42 x 46 threads)
Cut from 7 mesh canvas.

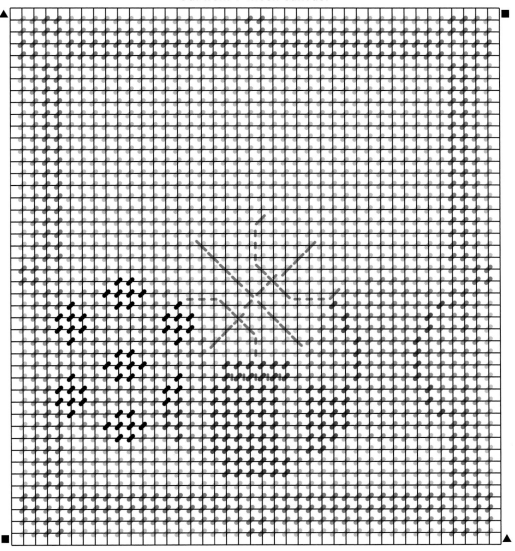

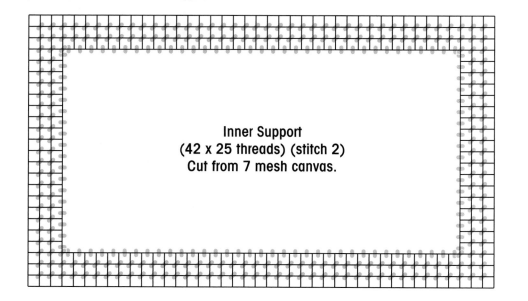

Inner Support
(42 x 25 threads) (stitch 2)
Cut from 7 mesh canvas.

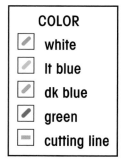

COLOR

✎	white
✎	lt blue
✎	dk blue
✎	green
▭	cutting line

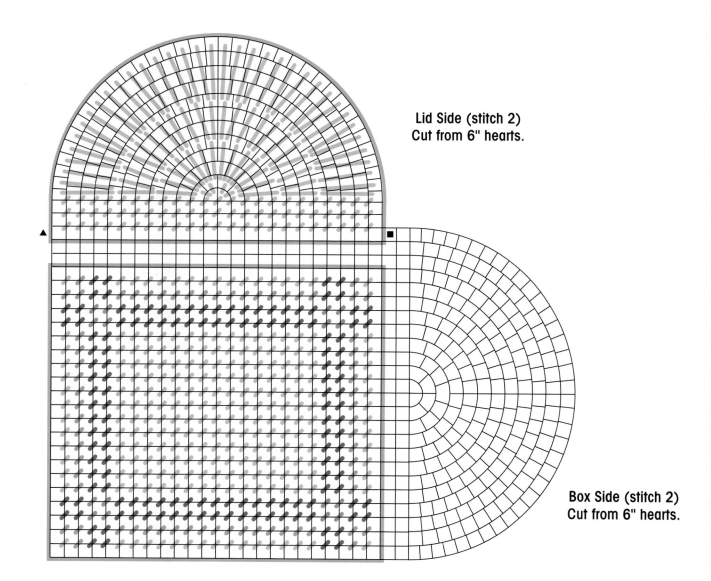

Lid Side (stitch 2)
Cut from 6" hearts.

Box Side (stitch 2)
Cut from 6" hearts.

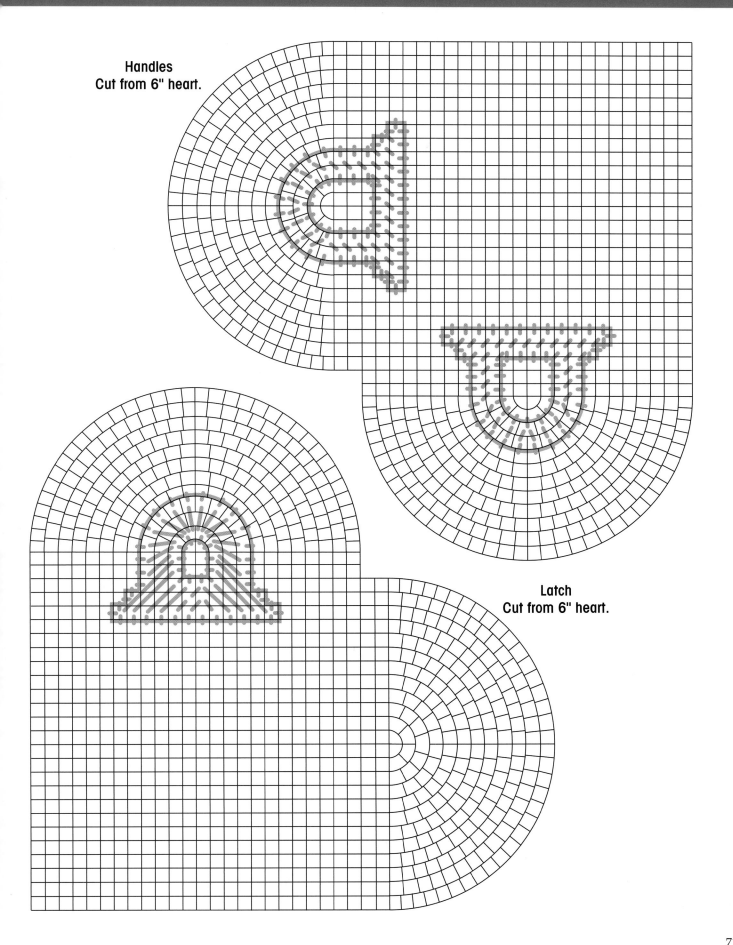

Handles
Cut from 6" heart.

Latch
Cut from 6" heart.

(Photo, page 65.)

Skill Level: Beginner

Size: 2³/₄"w x 2³/₄"h each

Supplies: Worsted weight yarn (refer to color key), four 3" Uniek® plastic canvas square shapes or one 10¹/₂" x 13¹/₂" sheet of clear 7 mesh plastic canvas, #16 tapestry needle, magnetic strip, and craft glue.

Stitches Used: Backstitch, Overcast Stitch, and Tent Stitch.

Instructions: Follow charts to cut and stitch Magnet pieces, working backstitches last. Glue a magnetic strip to back of each Magnet.

COLOR	
⟋	white - 10 yds
⟋	orange - 2 yds
⟋	red - 1 yd
⟋	green - 11 yds
⟋	lt brown - 2 yds
⟋	black - 1 yd
⟋	*white
⟋	*brown - 1 yd
▬	cutting line

*Use 2 plies of yarn.

Football (20 x 20 threads)

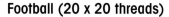
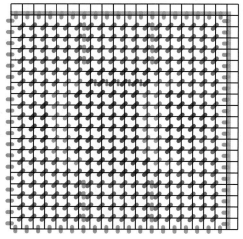

Soccer (20 x 20 threads)

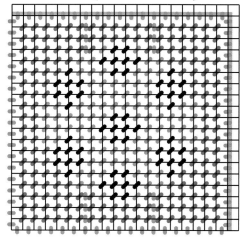

Baseball (20 x 20 threads)

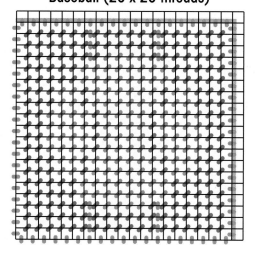

Basketball (20 x 20 threads)

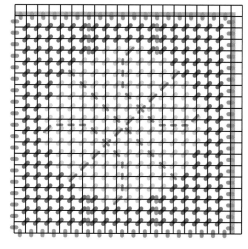

"Train-ing" Bank

Teaching the value of saving money will be child's play with this novel penny bank! Any kid will love this colorful locomotive, and watching coins disappear through the slot in the top will be pure fun!

(Photo, page 73.)

Skill Level: Intermediate

Size: 7½"w x 7"h x 3¼"d

Supplies: Worsted weight yarn (refer to color keys), one 10½" x 13½" sheet of clear 7 mesh plastic canvas, three 6" Uniek® plastic canvas heart shapes, six 3" Uniek® plastic canvas circle shapes, #16 tapestry needle, one ¾" paper fastener, 25mm gold liberty bell, and craft glue.

Stitches Used: Cross Stitch, Gobelin Stitch, Overcast Stitch, and Tent Stitch.

Instructions: Follow charts to cut and stitch Bank pieces. For Bottom, cut a piece of 7 mesh canvas 42 x 21 threads. Bottom is not worked. Using green overcast stitches, join short ends of Base, forming a cylinder. Center and tack Base to Bottom. Insert paper fastener in Door and Cab Back at ♦; secure fastener on wrong side of Cab Back. Using red overcast stitches, join Cab Front and Back to Cab Sides along long edges. Matching corners, join Cab Front, Back, and Sides to one end of Bottom. Using matching color overcast stitches, join Smoke Stack Sides along unworked edges. Tack Smoke Stack to Boiler at ★'s. Tack bell to center of Bell Holder. Tack short edges of Bell Holder to Boiler at ♥'s. Matching ✖'s, tack Reflector to Boiler Front. Using red overcast stitches, join Boiler Front to unworked edge of Boiler. Matching corners, join Boiler to Bottom. Join unworked edges of Boiler Front and Cow Catcher to Bottom, working through three layers of canvas. Securely tack Boiler to Cab Front. For each set of wheels, tack Drive Rod to Large Wheel and Small Wheel; glue Large Wheel to Cab Side and Small Wheel to Boiler. Securely tack Roof to Cab Front, Back, and Sides.

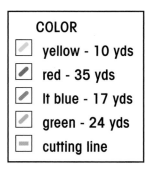

COLOR	
▨	yellow - 10 yds
▨	red - 35 yds
▨	lt blue - 17 yds
▨	green - 24 yds
▭	cutting line

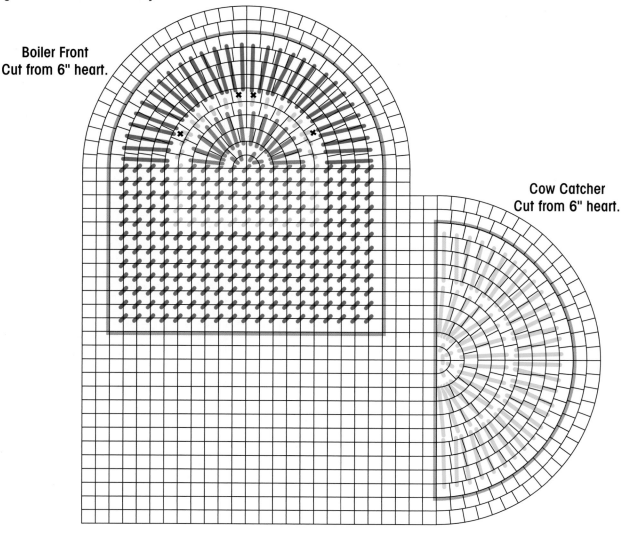

Boiler Front
Cut from 6" heart.

Cow Catcher
Cut from 6" heart.

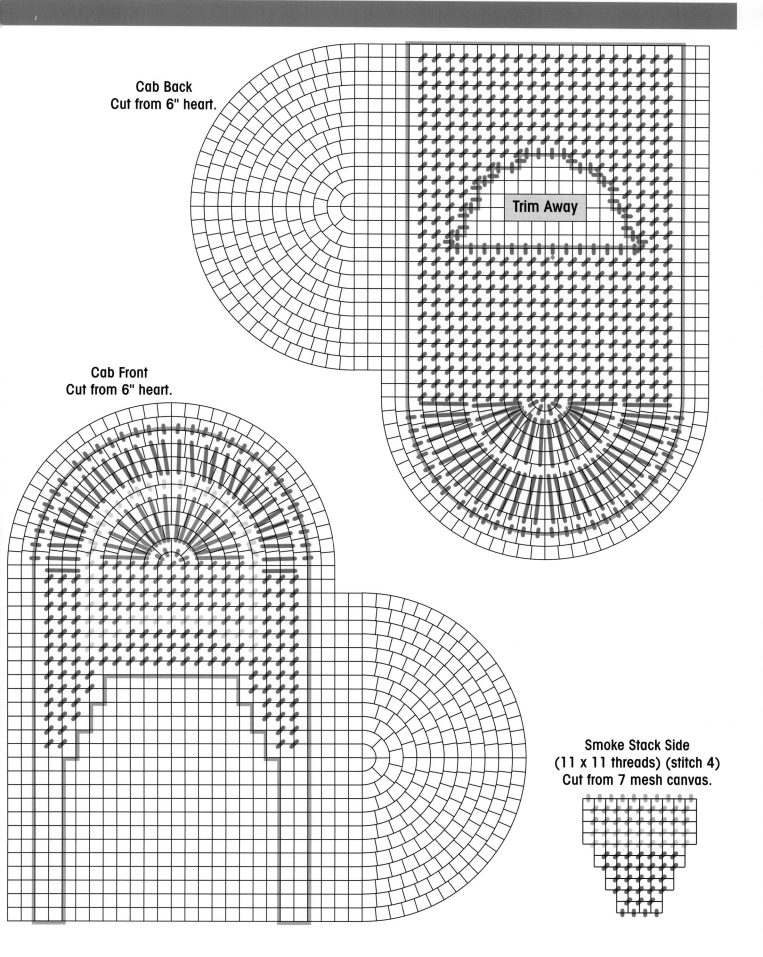

Cab Back
Cut from 6" heart.

Trim Away

Cab Front
Cut from 6" heart.

Smoke Stack Side
(11 x 11 threads) (stitch 4)
Cut from 7 mesh canvas.

Bell Holder (3 x 27 threads)
Cut from 7 mesh canvas.

Small Wheel (stitch 2)
Cut from 3" circles.
Use dk green overcast stitches to cover
unworked edges of Small Wheels.

Large Wheel (stitch 2)
Cut from 3" circles.
Use dk green overcast stitches to cover
unworked edges of Large Wheels.

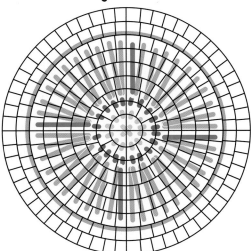

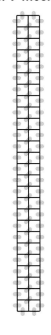

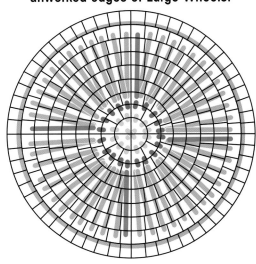

Drive Rod
(5 x 26 threads) (stitch 2)
Cut from 7 mesh canvas.

Door
Cut from 3" circle.
Use red overcast stitches to cover
unworked edges of Door.

Reflector
Cut from 3" circle.

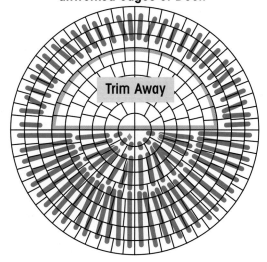

Trim Away

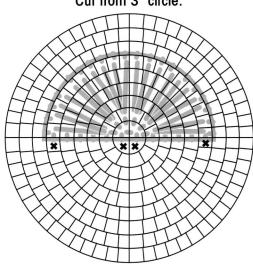

Base (51 x 8 threads)
Cut from 7 mesh canvas.

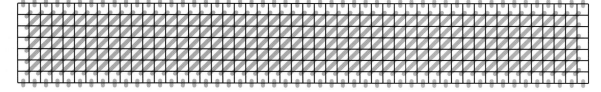

COLOR

 white - 2 yds

yellow

red

lt blue

blue - 15 yds

green

dk green - 12 yds

cutting line

Cab Side
(21 x 27 threads) (stitch 2)
Cut from 7 mesh canvas.

Boiler (21 x 57 threads)
Cut from 7 mesh canvas.

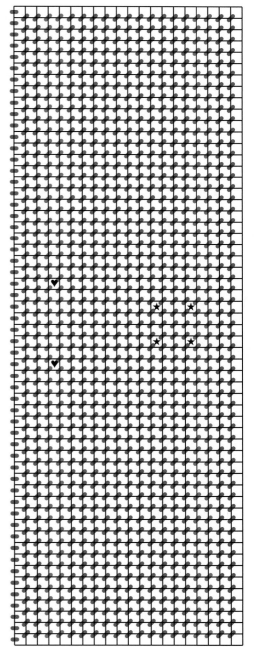

Roof (27 x 38 threads)
Cut from 7 mesh canvas.

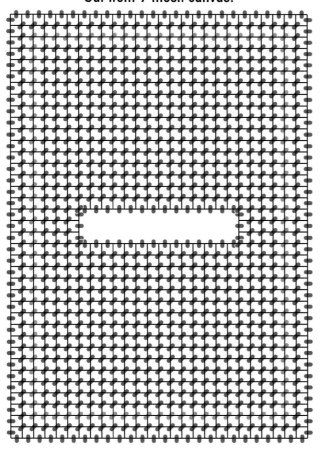

Celestial Sleepy-time Set

Baby will drift off to Dreamland with ease when this celestial sleepy-time set is used to decorate the nursery. A tissue box cover and a switch plate cover highlight the ensemble. The darling door sign will let guests know if it's naptime, while a happy moon-and-stars mobile orbits above the crib.

CELESTIAL SLEEPY-TIME SET

Skill Level: Intermediate

Supplies for entire set: Worsted weight yarn (refer to color keys), two $10^{1}/_{2}$" x $13^{1}/_{2}$" sheets of clear 7 mesh plastic canvas, three 9" Uniek® plastic canvas circle shapes, six 4" Uniek® plastic canvas circle shapes, thirteen 3" Uniek® plastic canvas circle shapes, seventeen 5" Uniek® plastic canvas star shapes, two 5" Uniek® plastic canvas hexagon shapes, #16 tapestry needle, six $^{1}/_{2}$" white pom-poms, white pearl cotton, 24" length of $^{1}/_{4}$"w white ribbon, and craft glue.

Stitches Used: Backstitch, Gobelin Stitch, Mosaic Stitch, Overcast Stitch, and Tent Stitch.

TISSUE BOX COVER

(Photo, page 78.)

Size: $6^{1}/_{4}$"w x $5^{3}/_{4}$"h x $4^{3}/_{4}$"d

(Fits a $4^{1}/_{4}$"w x $5^{1}/_{4}$"h x $4^{1}/_{4}$"d boutique tissue box.)

Instructions: Follow the charts here and on pgs. 82-85 to cut and stitch Tissue Box Cover Top, Tissue Box Cover Front/Back/Sides, Moon, Moon Hat Front, Moon Hat Back, Moon Cheek, Very Small Star, Yellow Star, Star Hat Front, Star Hat Back, and Tissue Box Cover Top Star, working backstitches last. Using blue overcast stitches, join Front and Back to Sides along long edges. Join Top to Front, Back, and Sides. Tack Top Star to Top. With wrong sides together, use aqua overcast stitches to join Moon Hat Front to Moon Hat Back. Slide Moon Hat over Moon; tack. Tack Moon Cheek to Moon; tack Moon to Front. With wrong sides together, use matching color overcast stitches to join Star Hat Front to Star Hat Back. Slide Star Hat over Yellow Star; tack. Tack Yellow Star and Very Small Star to Front. Glue pom-poms to Hats.

SWITCH PLATE COVER

(Photo, page 78.)

Size: 5"w x $7^{1}/_{4}$"h

Instructions: Follow the charts on pg[s]. 81-85 to cut and stitch Switch Pla[te] Cover, Moon, Moon Hat Front, Moo[n] Hat Back, Moon Cheek, Very Small Sta[r,] Yellow Star, Star Hat Front, and Star H[at] Back, working backstitches last. Wi[th] wrong sides together, use aqu[a] overcast stitches to join Moon Hat Fro[nt] to Moon Hat Back. Slide Moon Hat ov[er] Moon; tack. Tack Moon Cheek to Moo[n;] tack Moon to Switch Plate Cover. Wi[th] wrong sides together, use matchin[g] color overcast stitches to join Star H[at] Front to Star Hat Back. Slide Star H[at] over Yellow Star; tack. Tack Yellow St[ar] and Very Small Star to Switch Pla[te] Cover. Glue pom-poms to Hats.

Tissue Box Cover Front/Back/Sides
(32 x 38 threads) (stitch 4)
Cut from 7 mesh canvas.

Tissue Box Cover Top
(32 x 32 threads)
Cut from 7 mesh canvas.

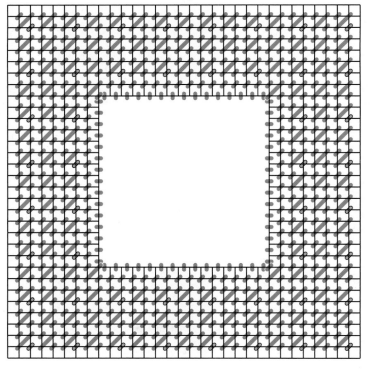

DOOR SIGN

(Photo, page 79.)

Size: 6¼"w x 10½"h

Instructions: Follow the charts on pgs. 81-85 to cut and stitch Door Sign, Moon, Moon Hat Front, Moon Hat Back, Moon Cheek, Very Small Star, Yellow Star, Star Hat Front, and Star Hat Back, working backstitches last. With wrong sides together, use aqua overcast stitches to join Moon Hat Front to Moon Hat Back. Slide Moon Hat over Moon; tack. Tack Moon Cheek to Moon; tack Moon to Door Sign. With wrong sides together, use matching color overcast stitches to join Star Hat Front to Star Hat Back. Slide Star Hat over Yellow Star; tack. Tack Yellow Star and Very Small Star to Door Sign. Glue pom-poms to hats.

COLOR	
⧄	white
⧄	blue

Door Sign (28 x 70 threads)
Cut from 7 mesh canvas.

Switch Plate Cover
(28 x 41 threads)
Cut from 7 mesh canvas.

Very Small Star
Stitch one for Tissue Box Cover.
Stitch one for Door Sign.
Stitch one for Switch Plate Cover.
Cut from 5" stars.
Use lt yellow overcast stitches to cover unworked edges of Very Small Stars.

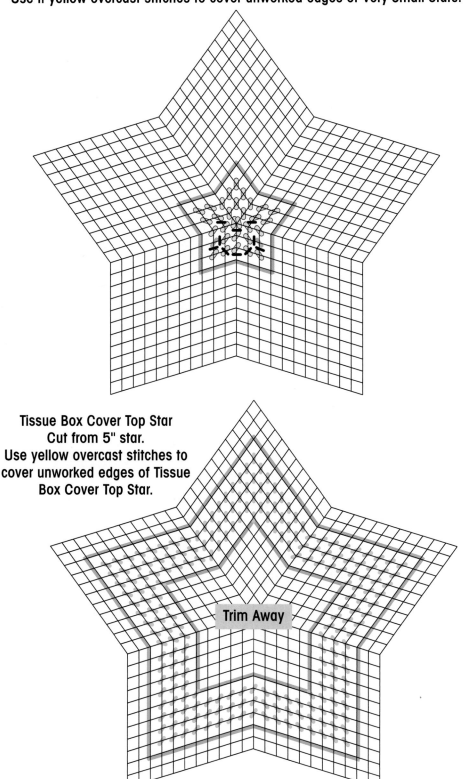

Tissue Box Cover Top Star
Cut from 5" star.
Use yellow overcast stitches to
cover unworked edges of Tissue
Box Cover Top Star.

Trim Away

MOBILE

(Photo, page 79.)
Size: 31"h
Instructions: Follow the charts o
pgs. 83-88 to cut and stitch Mobi
Moon Front, Mobile Moon Back, Mobi
Moon Hat Front, Mobile Moon H
Back, Mobile Cheeks, Mobile Pon
poms, Mobile Small Pom-poms, Mobi
Small Star Front/Backs, Mobile Larg
Star Front/Backs, and Mobile Star H
Front/Backs, working backstitches las
With wrong sides together and referrir
to photo for yarn color, use overca
stitches to join Mobile Moon Hat Fro
to Mobile Moon Hat Back alon
unworked edges. Tack Mobile Cheeks
Mobile Moon Front and Back. Wi
wrong sides together, use whi
overcast stitches to join Mobile Moc
Front to Mobile Moon Back. With wror
sides together, join unworked edges
Mobile Pom-poms. Slide Mobile Por
poms over Mobile Moon Hat Front ar
Back; tack. Slide Mobile Moon Hat ov
Mobile Moon; tack. For each Mobi
Small Star, match wrong sides and us
lt yellow overcast stitches to join Mobi
Small Star Front to Mobile Small St
Back. For each Mobile Large Sto
match wrong sides and use yello
overcast stitches to join Mobile Larg
Star Front to Mobile Large Star Bac
For each Mobile Star Hat, match wror
sides and use matching color overca
stitches to join Mobile Star Hat Front
Mobile Star Hat Back. With wrong side
together, use white overcast stitches
join unworked edges of Mobile Sma
Pom-poms. Slide Mobile Small Por
poms over Mobile Star Hat Front ar
Back; tack. Slide Mobile Star Hat ov
Mobile Large Star; tack. To assemb
Mobile, refer to Diagram on pg. 96 ar
cut lengths of pearl cotton sever
inches longer than each finished leng
shown on the Diagram. Tie pearl cotto
to pieces as shown in Diagram. F
hanger, thread ribbon through top
Mobile Moon; tie and trim ribbon ar
pearl cotton ends.

**Refer to pg. 96 for Mobile
Diagram.**

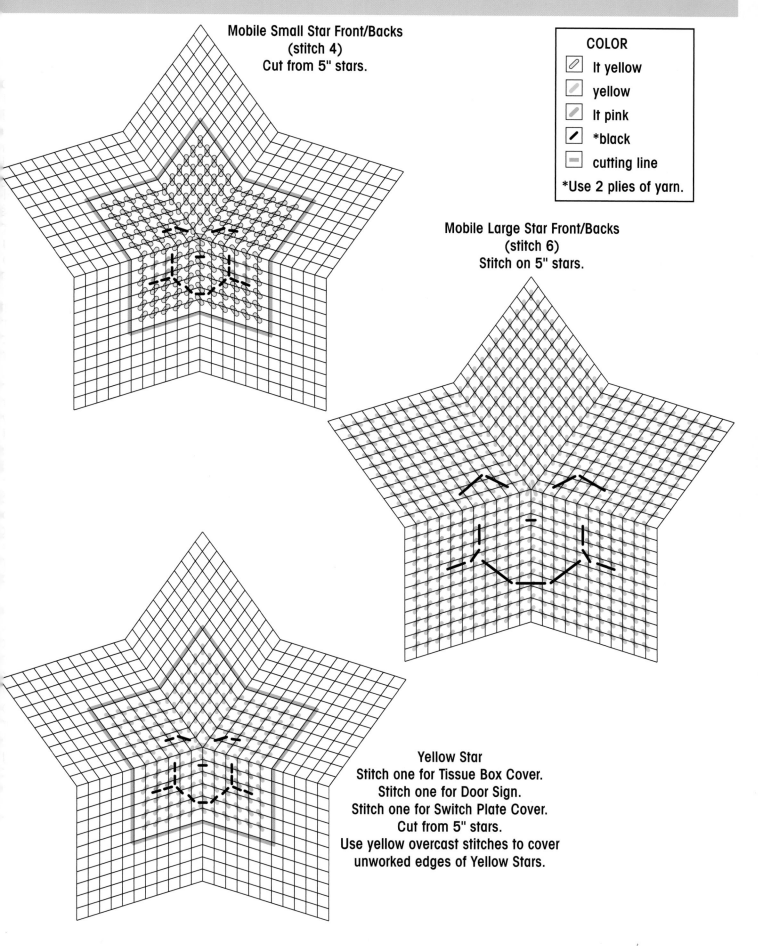

Mobile Small Star Front/Backs
(stitch 4)
Cut from 5" stars.

COLOR
It yellow
yellow
It pink
*black
cutting line
*Use 2 plies of yarn.

Mobile Large Star Front/Backs
(stitch 6)
Stitch on 5" stars.

Yellow Star
Stitch one for Tissue Box Cover.
Stitch one for Door Sign.
Stitch one for Switch Plate Cover.
Cut from 5" stars.
Use yellow overcast stitches to cover
unworked edges of Yellow Stars.

Mobile Small Pom-poms (stitch 6)
Cut from 3" circles.

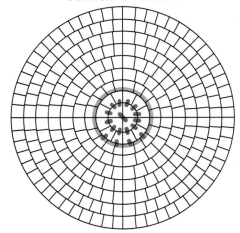

Moon Hat Front
Stitch one for Tissue Box Cover.
Stitch one for Door Sign.
Stitch one for Switch Plate Cover.
Cut from 4" circles.

Moon Hat Back
Cut one for Tissue Box Cover.
Cut one for Door Sign.
Cut one for Switch Plate Cover.
Cut from 4" circles.

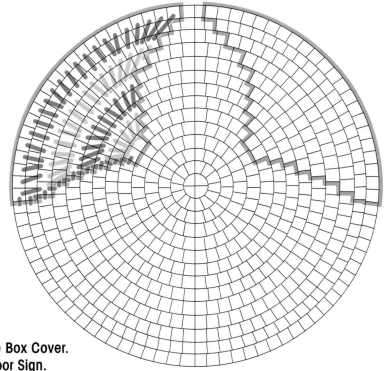

Star Hat Front/Back
Stitch one Front and cut one Back for Tissue Box Cover.
Stitch one Front and cut one Back for Door Sign.
Stitch one Front and cut one Back for Switch Plate Cover.
Cut from 5" hexagon.

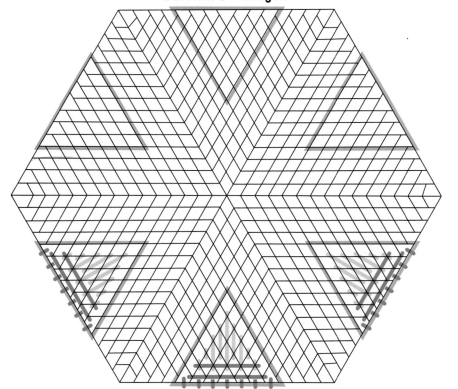

Moon Cheek
Stitch one for Tissue Box Cover.
Stitch one for Door Sign.
Stitch one for Switch Plate Cover.
Cut from 3" circles.
Use lt pink overcast stitches to cover unworked
edges of Moon Cheeks.

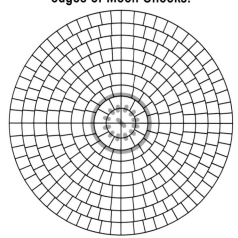

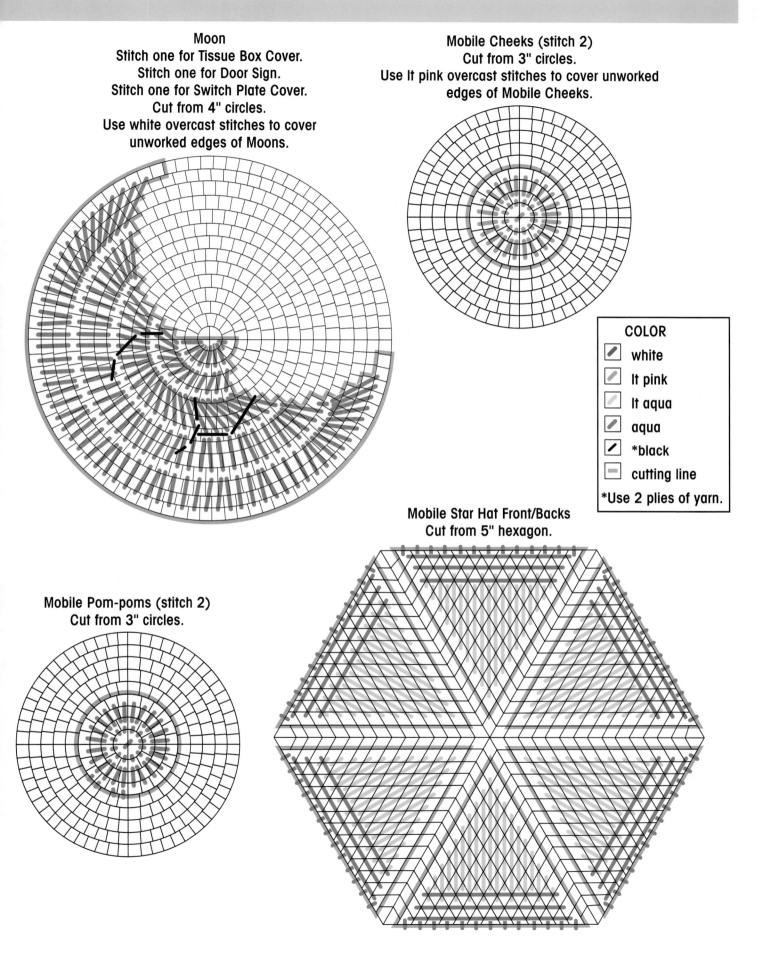

Moon
Stitch one for Tissue Box Cover.
Stitch one for Door Sign.
Stitch one for Switch Plate Cover.
Cut from 4" circles.
Use white overcast stitches to cover
unworked edges of Moons.

Mobile Cheeks (stitch 2)
Cut from 3" circles.
Use lt pink overcast stitches to cover unworked
edges of Mobile Cheeks.

COLOR

✏	white
✏	lt pink
✏	lt aqua
✏	aqua
✏	*black
▬	cutting line

*Use 2 plies of yarn.

Mobile Star Hat Front/Backs
Cut from 5" hexagon.

Mobile Pom-poms (stitch 2)
Cut from 3" circles.

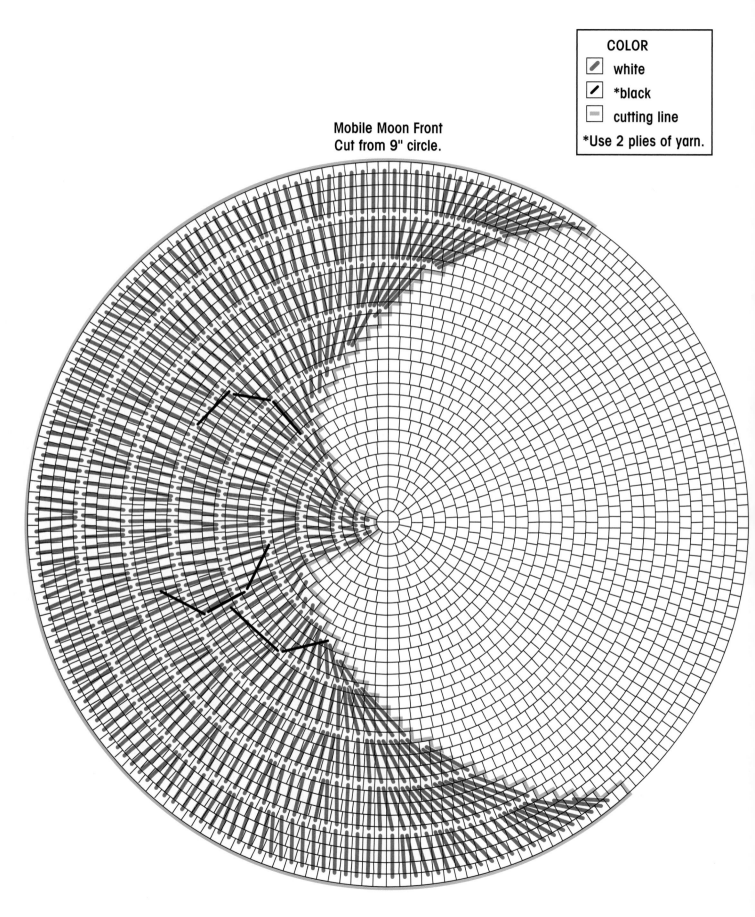

Mobile Moon Front
Cut from 9" circle.

COLOR
- ⟋ white
- ⟋ *black
- ▭ cutting line

*Use 2 plies of yarn.

**Mobile Moon Back
Cut from 9" circle.**

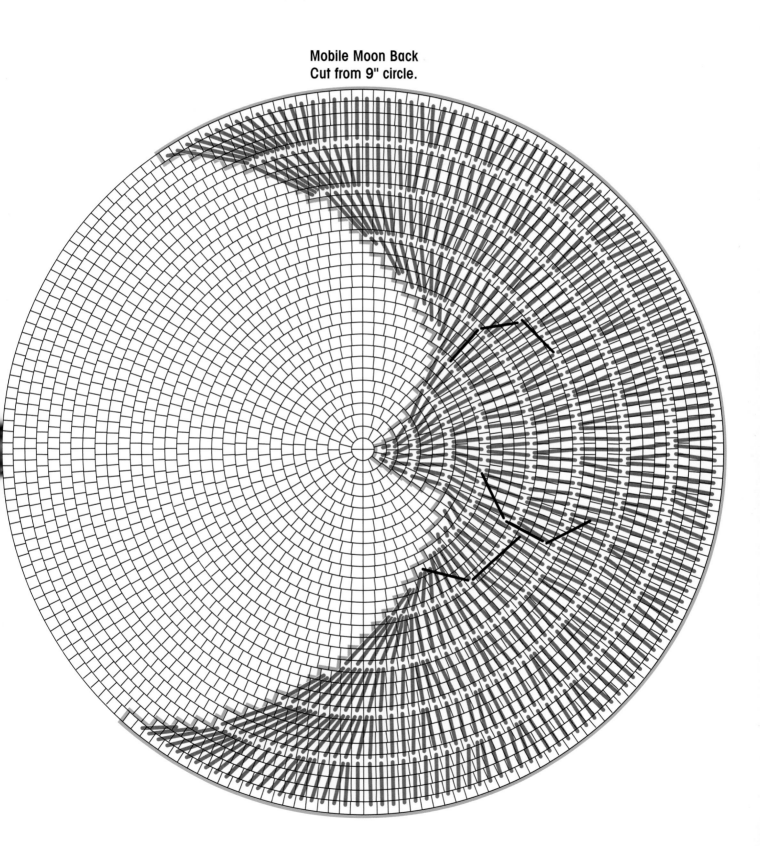

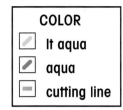

COLOR
- It aqua
- aqua
- cutting line

Mobile Moon Hat Front
Cut from 9" circle.

Mobile Moon Hat Back
Cut from 9" circle.

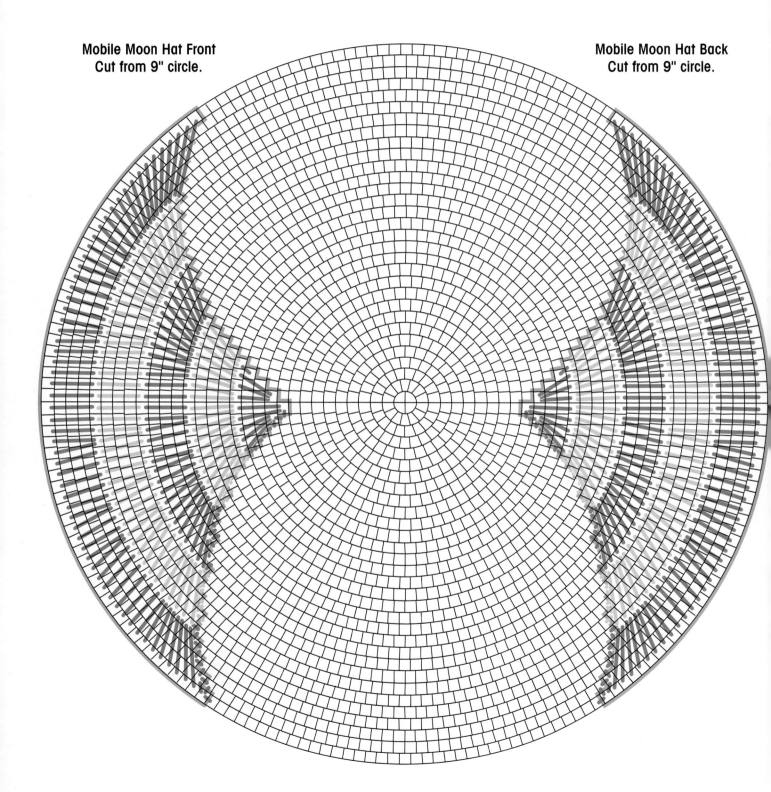

Sweet Attraction

If your family loves sweets, then attract them to your message center with these taste-tempting treat magnets! Looking good enough to eat, the clever stick-ups can be whipped up in a jiffy.

(Photo, page 89.)
Skill Level: Beginner
Popsicle Size: 1³/₄"w x 4¹/₄"h each
Cupcake Size: 2³/₄"w x 3"h each
Supplies: Worsted weight yarn (refer to color key), eight 6" Uniek® plastic canvas heart shapes, #16 tapestry needle, magnetic strip, and craft glue.
Stitches Used: Gobelin Stitch, Overcast Stitch, and Tent Stitch.
Instructions: Follow charts to cut and stitch Magnet pieces. Tack a Cherry to the back of each Cupcake. Glue a magnetic strip to back of each Magnet.

COLOR	
✎	white - 1 yd
✎	red - 1 yd
✎	lt brown - 6 yds
✎	Popsicle® color - 3 yds of each color
✎	icing color - 3 yds of each color
▭	cutting line

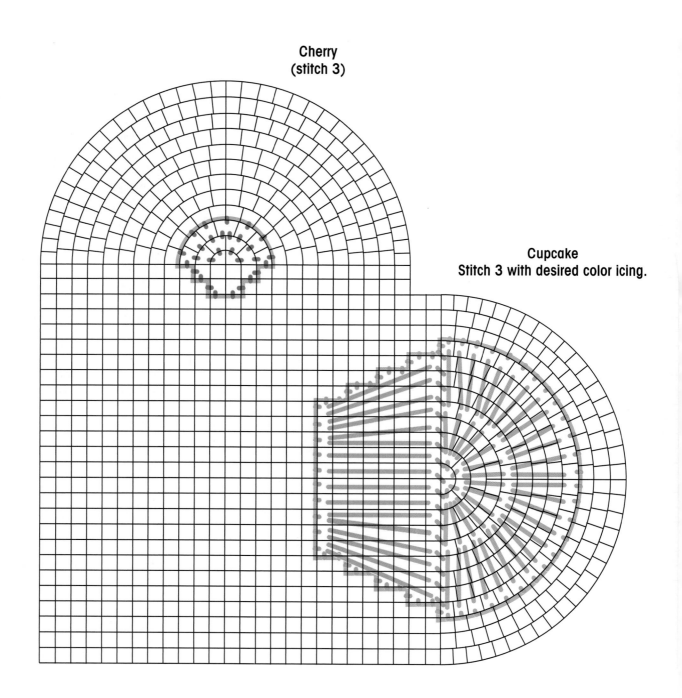

Cherry
(stitch 3)

Cupcake
Stitch 3 with desired color icing.

Popsicle®
Stitch 2 with desired colors.

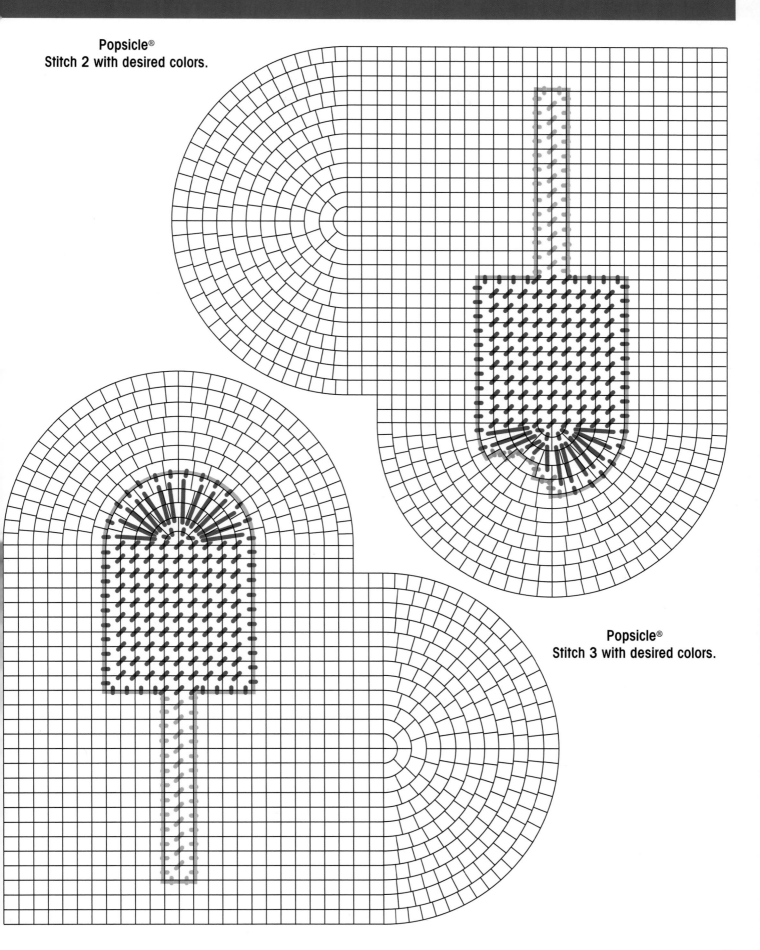

Popsicle®
Stitch 3 with desired colors.

GENERAL INSTRUCTIONS

SELECTING PLASTIC CANVAS

Regardless of the shape, plastic canvas is a molded material that consists of "threads" and "holes," but the threads aren't actually "threads" since the canvas is not woven. Project instructions often refer to the threads, especially when cutting out plastic canvas pieces. The holes are the spaces between the threads. The Stitch Diagrams, pages 95-96, will refer to holes when explaining where to place your needle to make a stitch.

TYPES OF CANVAS

The plastic canvas used in this book includes 10¹/₂" x 13¹/₂" sheets of 7 mesh plastic canvas and a variety of canvas shapes. We used Uniek® brand shapes for our 3" and 4" squares, 3", 4", 6", and 9" circles, 6" hearts, 5" stars, and 5" hexagons. Darice® brand was used for the 3" hearts.

Most plastic canvas is clear, but colored 10¹/₂" x 13¹/₂" sheets of 7 mesh plastic are also available. Colored canvas is ideal when you don't want to stitch the entire background. We used Darice® florescent yellow canvas for our Bug-Catcher's Box on pg. 28.

AMOUNT OF CANVAS

The project supply list will tell you how much canvas and/or how many shapes will be needed to complete the project. As a general rule, it is better to buy too much canvas and have leftovers than to run out of canvas before you finish your project.

SELECTING NEEDLES
TYPES OF NEEDLES

A blunt needle called a tapestry needle is used for stitching on plastic canvas. Tapestry needles are sized by numbers; the higher the number, the smaller the needle. The correct size needle to use depends on the canvas mesh size and the yarn thickness. The needle should be small enough to allow the threaded needle to pass through the canvas holes easily. The eye of the needle should be large enough to allow yarn to be threaded easily. If the eye is too small, the yarn will wear thin and may break. You will find the recommended needle size listed in the supply section of each project. A #16 tapestry needle is used for all of the projects in this book.

SELECTING YARN

We have a few hints to help you choose the perfect yarns for your project.

COLORS

Your project will tell you what yarn colors you will need. Choose colors and brands to suit your needs and your taste.

YARN

All of the projects in this book were stitched with worsted weight yarn. This yarn may be found in acrylic, wool, wool blends, and a variety of other fiber contents. Worsted weight yarn is the most popular yarn used for 7 mesh plastic canvas because one strand covers the canvas very well. This yarn is inexpensive and comes in a wide

range of colors. Worsted weight yarn has four plies that are twisted together to form one strand. When the instructions call for two plies of yarn, you will remove two plies of yarn and stitch with the remaining two plies.

WORKING WITH PLASTIC CANVAS
CUTTING CANVAS SHEETS

Throughout this book, the lines of the canvas will be referred to as threads. To cut plastic canvas pieces accurately from 10¹/₂" x 13¹/₂" sheets, count threads (not holes) as shown in Fig. 1.

Fig. 1

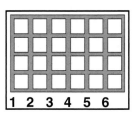

Before cutting out your pieces, note the thread count located above the chart for each piece. The thread count tells you the number of threads in the width and the height of the canvas piece. It can be helpful to follow the thread count to count out a rectangle the specified size before cutting out your shape. Then, remembering to count threads, not holes, follow the chart to trim the rectangle into the desired shape.

CUTTING CANVAS SHAPES

Our charts for shapes have a colored cutting line (shown in **Fig. 2** as a dark grey line). You will need to cut on the side of the line that will give you a complete shape within the stitching area **(Fig. 3)**. Do not cut along the middle of the plastic canvas thread when cutting out squares, circles, or hearts.

The star and hexagon shapes are a bit different; you can cut along the middle of some plastic canvas threads because the threads are actually double and have indentions for you to cut **(Fig. 4)**.

Sometimes the project instructions will tell you to trim away 3 (or some other number) of threads from the outer edge. Count that many threads and trim away those threads **(Fig. 5)**.

Fig. 2

Fig. 4

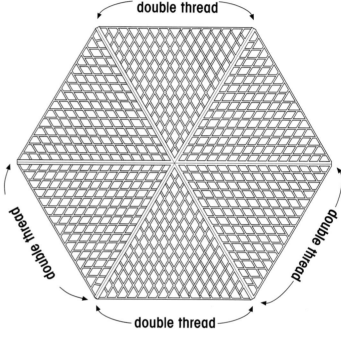

double thread

double thread

double thread

double thread

Fig. 3

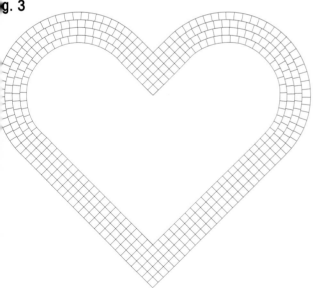

Fig. 5

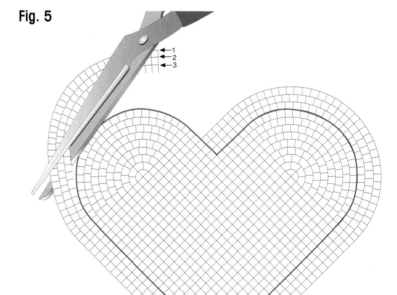

CUTTING TIPS

You may want to use an overhead projector pen to outline the piece on the canvas before cutting it out. Before you begin stitching, be sure to remove all markings with a damp towel. Any markings could rub off on the yarn as you stitch.

A good pair of household scissors is recommended for cutting plastic canvas. However, a craft knife is helpful when cutting out small areas. When using a craft knife, protect the table below your canvas with a layer of cardboard or a magazine.

When cutting canvas, cut as close to the thread as possible without cutting into the thread. If you don't cut close enough, "nubs" or "pickets" will be left on the edge of your canvas. Make sure to cut all nubs from the canvas before you begin to stitch because nubs will snag the yarn and are difficult to cover.

Anytime a 3" or 4" square is listed in the supplies, a sheet of 7 mesh canvas may be substituted. Simply follow the thread count above the chart to cut out the piece.

THREADING YOUR NEEDLE

Several brands of yarn-size needle threaders are available at your local craft store. Here are a couple of methods that will make threading your needle easier without a purchased threader.

FOLD METHOD

First, sharply fold the end of yarn over your needle; then remove needle. Keeping the fold sharp, push the needle onto the yarn **(Fig. 6)**.

Fig. 6

THREAD METHOD

Fold a 5" piece of sewing thread in half, forming a loop. Insert loop of thread through the eye of your needle **(Fig. 7)**. Insert yarn through the loop and pull the thread back through your needle, pulling yarn through at the same time.

Fig. 7

READING THE CHART

Whenever possible the drawing on the chart looks like the completed stitch. For example, a tent stitch on the chart is drawn diagonally across one intersection of threads just like a tent stitch looks when stitched on your canvas. A symbol will be used on the chart when a stitch, such as a French knot, cannot be clearly drawn. If you have difficulty determining how a particular stitch should be worked, refer to the list of stitches in the project information and the Stitch Diagrams on pages 95-96.

READING THE COLOR KEY

Color keys are given with the project. The keys indicate the color used for each stitch on the chart. For example, when white yarn is represented by a grey line in the color key, all grey stitches on the chart should be stitched using white yarn.

Additional information may also be included in the color key, such as the number of plies of yarn to use when working a particular stitch.

STITCHING THE DESIGN

Securing the First Stitch - Don't knot the end of your yarn before you begin stitching. Instead, begin each length of yarn by coming up from the wrong side of the canvas and leaving a 1" - 2" tail on the wrong side. Hold this tail against the canvas and work the first few stitches over the tail. When secure, clip the tail close to your stitched piece. Clipping the tail closely is important because long tails can become tangled in future stitches or show through to the right side of the canvas.

Using Even Tension - Keep your stitching tension consistent, with each stitch lying flat and even on the canvas. Pulling or yanking the yarn causes the tension to be too tight, and you will be able to see through your project. Loose tension is caused by not pulling the yarn firmly enough; consequently, the yarn will not lie flat on the canvas.

nding Your Stitches - After you've completed all of the stitches of one olor in an area, end your stitching by unning your needle under several titches on the back of the stitched iece. To keep the tails of the yarn from nowing through or becoming tangled future stitches, trim the end of the arn close to the stitched piece.

OINING PIECES

traight Edges - The most common method of assembling stitched pieces is ining two or more pieces of canvas ong a straight edge using overcast itches. Place one piece on top of the her with right or wrong sides together. ake sure the edges being joined are ven, then stitch the pieces together rough all layers.

acking - To tack pieces, run your eedle under the backs of some stitches one stitched piece to secure the arn. Then run your needle through the anvas or under the stitches on the ece to be tacked in place. The idea is securely attach your pieces without ur tacking stitches showing.

aded Areas - The shaded area is part a chart that has colored shading on o of it. Shaded areas usually mean at all the stitches in that area are used join pieces of canvas. Do not work e stitches in a shaded area until your oject instructions say you should.

STITCH DIAGRAMS

Unless otherwise indicated, bring threaded needle up at 1 and all odd numbers and down at 2 and all even numbers.

BACKSTITCH

This stitch is worked over completed stitches to outline or define **(Fig. 8)**. It is sometimes worked over more than one thread.

Fig. 8

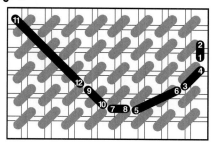

CROSS STITCH

This stitch is composed of two stitches **(Fig. 9)**. The top stitch of each cross must always be made in the same direction. The number of intersections may vary according to the chart.

Fig. 9

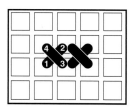

FRENCH KNOT

Bring needle up through hole. Wrap yarn around needle once and insert needle in same hole **(Fig. 10)**. Tighten knot as close to the canvas as possible as you pull the needle and yarn back through canvas.

Fig. 10

GOBELIN STITCH

This basic straight stitch is worked over two or more threads or intersections. The number of threads or intersections may vary according to the chart **(Fig. 11)**.

Fig. 11

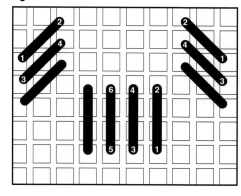

LAZY DAISY STITCH

Bring needle up at 1, make a loop and go down at 1 again **(Fig. 12)**. Come up at 2, keeping yarn below needle's point. Pull needle through and secure loop by bringing yarn over loop and going down at 2.

Fig. 12

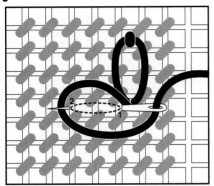

MOSAIC STITCH

This three-stitch pattern forms small squares **(Fig. 13)**.

Fig. 13

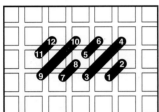

OVERCAST STITCH

This stitch covers the edge of the canvas and joins pieces of canvas **(Fig. 14)**. It may be necessary to go through the same hole more than once to get even coverage on the edge, especially at the corners.

Fig. 14

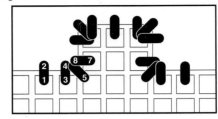

TENT STITCH

This stitch is worked in horizontal or vertical rows over one intersection as shown in **Fig. 15**. Refer to **Fig. 16** to work the reversed tent stitch.

Fig. 15

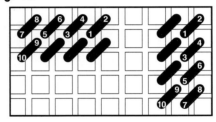

Fig. 16

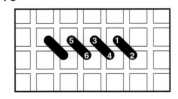

WASHING INSTRUCTIONS

If you used washable yarn for all your stitches, you may hand was plastic canvas projects in warn wat with a mild soap. Do not rub or scru stitches; this will cause the yarn to fuz Do not dry-clean or put your stitch pieces in a clothes dryer. Allow piec to air dry and trim any fuzz with a sm pair of sharp scissors or a sweat shaver.

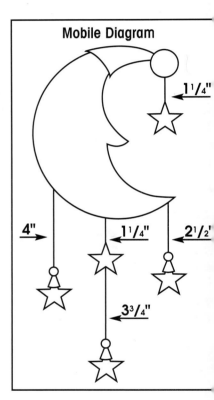

Mobile Diagram

Instructions tested and cover items made Kandi Ashford, Toni Bowden, Juanita Crisw Lylln Guth, Carlene Hodge, Mary Kennemur, Linda Rogers-Peters.

Plastic canvas shapes provided courtesy of Uniek®.